rororo sprachen
Herausgegeben von Ludwig Moos

Erfolgreiche Besprechungen jeder Art, ob Verhandlungen mit Lieferanten, Konferenzen in Planung, Vertrieb und Produktion oder Auftritte vor Kunden und auf Kongressen, verlangen ein klares sprachliches Konzept. *Get Through at Meetings* vermittelt in einer lockeren Mischung aus Dialogen, Jokes und Übungen alles, was Sie dazu brauchen. Es macht vertraut mit den Redemitteln, mit denen sich Meetings elegant eröffnen, leiten, unterbrechen, in ihrer Richtung ändern und schließen lassen. Es vermittelt die Sprache, mit der Sie sich selbst, Ihre Ideen und Produkte präsentieren können. Und es verleiht Ihnen das taktische und sprachliche Vermögen zum Verhandeln. Die Toncassette zum Buch (60266) verrät, wie sich das alles anhört, und schult im Sprechen.

Dr. René Bosewitz ist Native Speaker und bereitet in einer deutschen Zweigstelle der Londoner Chamber of Commerce Firmenangehörige auf einschlägige sprachliche Prüfungen vor. Er trainiert zudem seit vielen Jahren Manager aus Banken und Industrie in Buisness English. Mit Robert Kleinschroth hat er bei rororo sprachen *Joke Your Way Through English Grammar* (18527) und *Joke by Joke to Conversation* (18795) veröffentlicht.

Robert Kleinschroth unterrichtet Englisch am Gymnasium und an der Universität Heidelberg. Er hat zwanzig Jahre Praxis in der Erwachsenenbildung und leitete fünfzehn Jahre lang die Sprachabteilung eines Großunternehmens. Robert Kleinschroth hat zusammen mit Dieter Maupai *La Grammaire en s'amusant* (18714) verfaßt und außerdem *La Conversation en s'amusant* (18873) sowie *Sprachen lernen* (60842) geschrieben.

In der Reihe *Business English* sind von beiden Autoren außerdem erschienen: *Manage in English* (60137), *Better than the Boss* (60138), *How to Phone Effectively* (60139), *Drop Them a Line* (60261, mit Bryan Hemming), *Test Your Management Skills* (60260), *Let's Go International* (60267), *Check Your Language Level* (60268), *Business English from A to Z* (60269, mit Bryan Hemming), *The Way Things Work* (60369), *How to Read the Business Press* (60506), *Small Talk for Big Business* (60439), *Business by Jokes* (60721), *Sell like Hell* (60722), *Master Your Business Phrases* (60725), *Spice up Your Speeches* (60804), *Get to Grips with Company English* (60845) und *Better Your Business English* (60846).

RENÉ BOSEWITZ / ROBERT KLEINSCHROTH

GET THROUGH AT MEETINGS

BUSINESS ENGLISH

FÜR KONFERENZEN UND PRÄSENTATIONEN

Rowohlt

rororo

Wir danken Frau Ortrud Grimm vielmals für ihre Hilfe
bei der Erstellung des Manuskripts.
Ohne sie hätten wir es wohl nicht geschafft.

4. Auflage April 2002

Originalausgabe
Veröffentlicht im Rowohlt Taschenbuch Verlag GmbH,
Reinbek bei Hamburg, April 1997

Umschlaggestaltung Barbara Hanke
Illustration Cathrin Günther
Layout Anne Drude und Alexander Urban
Satz OCR-A und Stone, PostScript Linotype Library,
QuarkXPress 3.31 (Dolev 800)
Druck und Bindung Clausen & Bosse, Leck
Printed in Germany
ISBN 3 499 60262 8

Inhalt

Gebrauchsanweisung

Welcher Geschäftsmann will nicht gute Geschäfte machen und Geld verdienen? Gute Geschäfte sind das Ergebnis von guten Verhandlungen und gekonnten Präsentationen, die in gute Verträge münden. Wir sind eine Exportnation, deshalb kommen wichtige Verträge mit dem Ausland nach Besprechungen, Präsentationen und Verhandlungen in englischer Sprache zustande. Dieses Buch will Ihnen dabei helfen. Wir haben versucht, das Nützliche mit dem Angenehmen zu verbinden. Sie sollen lernen und dabei etwas zum Schmunzeln haben. Dafür sorgen unsere humorvollen Dialoge, Witze und geistreichen Zitate. Letztere haben alle mit dem Thema des Buches zu tun.
Eine Gruppe von englischen und deutschen Lehrern, die des Unterrichtens müde geworden sind, gründet eine Firma. Sie wollen internationale Patente vermarkten. Skurrile Erfinder bieten groteske Erfindungen an (die mit wenigen Ausnahmen nicht unserer Phantasie entsprungen sind, sondern für die es tatsächlich Patentschriften gibt). Die frischgebackenen Unternehmer diskutieren ihre Projekte in typisch englischen Besprechungen und stellen sie ihren potentiellen Kunden vor, was nicht ohne Pleiten und Pannen abgeht. Aus ihren Fehlern sollen Sie lernen. Dabei werden Sie nach und nach auch die sprachlichen Redemittel der englischen Konferenz- und Präsentationssprache erwerben und in abwechslungsreichen, kurzen Übungen festigen, deren Lösungen Sie im Anhang finden. Und wenn Sie wissen wollen, wie das Ganze klingt, wählen Sie die Ausgabe mit der Audio-CD oder kaufen die Kassette zum Buch.
Jedes Kapitel schließt mit einem Follow-up-Text, der Sie an Strategien und Techniken erinnert und vor Fehlern bewahren möchte. Hier erfahren Sie auch etwas über die Konferenzkultur wichtiger Geschäftspartner (England, USA, Japan, Frankreich, Italien, Spanien).
Im Anhang haben wir, nach Situationen geordnet, rund 700 Redewendungen zusammengestellt, mit denen Sie sich gezielt auf Besprechungen vorbereiten können.
Das Buch eignet sich auch für den Einsatz im Kursunterricht. Im Anschluß an die fünfzehn Kapitel machen wir unseren Kollegen Vorschläge zu Rollenspielen und Simulationen.

So sind die Kapitel aufgebaut

Our story: Eine *storyline,* erzählt in Dialogen, bildet den Rahmen zu den einzelnen Episoden. Haben Sie die Version mit der CD erstanden oder die Kassette zum Buch gekauft, dann erzielen Sie den größten Lernerfolg, wenn Sie in drei Schritten vorgehen:

1. Sie lesen den Dialog.
2. Sie **hören** und lesen mit.
3. Sie hören ohne den Text.

V **Vocabulary:** Die Wortschatzliste sorgt dafür, daß Sie beim Lesen oder Hören alles verstehen.

Focus: Die im Dialog verwendeten Redemittel *(speech functions)* der Konferenz- und Präsentationssprache, auf die es im Kapitel ankommt (jedes Kapitel widmet sich einem Thema), finden Sie in einer Übersicht im Übungsteil *(result of our word watching)*. Falls Sie einmal ein Übersetzung benötigen, schlagen Sie im thematisch geordneten Gesamtverzeichnis im Anhang nach.

B **Brain work:** Eine Batterie von Übungen *(tasks)* prüft und festigt das Textverstehen und die Redewendungen unter verschiedenen Aspekten. Um den vollen Gewinn aus diesem Buch zu ziehen, ist es wichtig, daß Sie Sinn und Zusammenspiel der einzelnen Übung verstehen. Deshalb empfehlen wir die nächste Seite Ihrer besonderen Aufmerksamkeit.

L **Language box:** Der Ton macht die Musik. Man kann ein und derselben Äußerung ganz unterschiedliche Noten geben. Dies geschieht mit grammatischen und stilistischen Mitteln, die Sie in der Box finden. Oft schließt sich die Übung **Mind your manners** an.

(F) **Follow-up:** Die Kapitel schließen entweder mit einer Manöverkritik der Episode oder mit einem Lesetext ab, der Ihnen Tips zu Dingen gibt, die man in Besprechungen und Präsentationen tun oder lieber lassen sollte. Auch auf die Besonderheiten der Konferenzkultur einzelner Länder gehen wir hier ein.

Time for a smile and Food for thought: Ausgesuchte Witze und geistreiche Zitate zum Thema sorgen dafür, daß Sie bei der Lektüre das Lächeln nicht vergessen.

Und so sehen die Übungen aus

Im **Brain work** – so heißt unsere Übungsbatterie – lernen Sie mit Methode. Die Übungen *(tasks)* sind kurz, abwechslungsreich und lernpsychologisch aufeinander abgestimmt. Die drei ehernen Gesetze der Lernpsychologie lauten:

1. Wir lernen und vergessen.
2. Wir lernen nur, wenn wir wiederholen.
3. Wiederholungen sind nur sinnvoll, wenn wir unter immer neuen Gesichtspunkten wiederholen.

Diesen Gesetzen haben wir bei der Auswahl und der Anordnung der Übungen Rechnung getragen. Auf die Übungen haben wir besondere Sorgfalt verwendet. *Kiss (keep it short, sweet)* ist unser Motto.

(B) **Brain work** umfaßt, in unterschiedlicher Mischung, meist vier bis sechs Übungstypen:

Word watch (or **Find the function**): Diese Übung möchte Ihre Aufmerksamkeit auf den besonderen sprachlichen Gesichtspunkt *(Focus)* eines jeden Kapitels lenken. Die Lösung finden Sie auf eine der nächsten Seiten desselben Kapitels.

Brain test: Diese Übung schult Ihr Lese- und Hörverstehen. Sie haben den Text gelesen (und angehört, wenn Sie die Audioversion des Buches haben).
Nun testen wir Ihr Gedächtnis, indem wir Ihnen zu jeder Frage drei Antworten vorlegen, von denen eine oder zwei richtig sind. Sie haben die Wahl.

Match work: Match work ist eine Zuordnungsübung. Sie wiederholen die in *Word watch* gefundenen Redemittel durch Ordnen. Mit den *speech functions of meetings and presentations* verfolgt der Sprecher ein Ziel. Er will unterbrechen, vorschlagen oder überzeugen. Sie sollen diese Ziele den Redemitteln zuordnen. Diese werden in der nächsten Übung unter einem neuen Aspekt gefestigt. Sie lernen durch Ordnen.

Patch work: Flickwerk haben wir diese Übung genannt – eine Wiederholung unter neuem Gesichtspunkt. Die *patches* sind Schlüsselwörter aus den *speech functions* und sollen sinngemäß in diese eingesetzt werden. Sie lernen durch Ergänzen.

Form and function: Wir legen Ihnen einige Redemittel für *meetings oder presentations* vor, und Sie identifizieren deren Funktionen. Sie wiederholen unter einem neuen Gesichtspunkt.

Degrees of politeness/emphasis etc.: Ein und dieselbe Redeabsicht kann auf verschiedene Art und Weise verwirklicht werden und kann bei den Zuhörern ganz unterschiedliche Reaktionen auslösen. Auf diese Nuancen soll Sie die Übung aufmerksam machen.

Mind your manners: Dies ist eine Wiederholungs- und Transformationsübung. Wir zeigen Ihnen, wie Sie eine Aussage direkt, indirekt, abgeschwächt, höflich oder mit Nachdruck vorbringen. Sie tun desgleichen an weiteren Beispielen.

Word power: Sie sollten immer mehrere Pfeile im Köcher haben. Mit dieser Übung erweitern Sie den im Kapitel erworbenen Sprachschatz. Ein Argument, einen Gedanken kann man auf ganz verschiedene Art und Weise ausdrücken. Wir geben Ihnen bereits bekannte *speech functions* vor, und Sie ordnen jeweils aus einem Angebot gleichbedeutende Wendungen zu. Sie lernen durch Suchen und Finden.

Wegweiser zu den Redemitteln

Redemittel für Vorsitzende

Meinungen äußern

Argumente gekonnt vorbringen

Einen Sprecher unterbrechen

Gegenargumente und Widerspruch

Unklarheiten klären, Mißverständnisse vermeiden

Beeinflussen, Überreden, Überzeugen

Konferenzkultur anderer Länder

Mixing business with pleasure

CONTENTS

Time for a smile

"Why did you walk out in the middle of the speech?" demanded the company chairman of one of his senior executives[1]. "It was an important meeting of shareholders[2] and you chose the most crucial[3] moment to walk out when I had been speaking for only forty minutes."
"I'm sorry, sir," replied the senior executive, "but it was nothing personal. I was just sleepwalking[4]."

1 leitender Angestellter 2 Aktionär 3 kritisch 4 schlafwandeln

Mixing business with pleasure

Well, where did it all begin? Nobody is actually sure who had the idea first. Anyway, once upon a time, two friends were sitting in a Heidelberg pub. They were discussing forming a company since they were in desperate need of money with taxes going up and the standard of living going down. But what to sell? What should they do? They both had good contacts to patent departments of major companies – and they had ideas.
Now let's listen in on a conversation between Norbert Kleinstück, his friends call him Nob or Nobby **(N)**, Ron Bossybitch, his enemies call him Bossy Ronald **(R)**, and William **(W)**, owner of the pub.

(In a pub; clattering of pots)

R: Well, now that the waiter's gone I'd like to say I'm certainly glad you've decided to come in with me on this project, Nobby. It's time for you to find out what it's like in the real world.

N: I know you think I'm lazy because I'm a Beamter. But you also know that I myself put a lot of work in, I ...

R: Nob, if I could break in a minute. I know you well enough! Anyway you're a workaholic or we wouldn't even be thinking of this idea of a company in addition to our normal work. And I ...

N: *(Banging his knife on his plate)* Hang on! We know all that! Let's keep on track! Our company. What are we able to do? Why ... ?

R: Please let me finish my sentence. Afterwards I'll answer your questions. Listen, I know it won't be easy. But we both have a lot of contacts to industry here. We've got no money! We can't produce anything. It's all too costly. We ...

N: I know your brain is racing, Ron, but could I just interrupt you a moment? What are you talking about? Do you really want to found a company?

You may wonder why the characters in our story are speaking English in the middle of Germany. Well, some are English, others English teachers. In industry a lot of the business goes on in English. More and more companies are introducing English as their company language, at least at the higher levels. Yours might, too. Just use your imaginations!

R: Nob! Are you getting old? *(Norbert coughing and choking)*. We discussed it last week. Of course we do!

N: I'm not sure we actually ...

R: Hang on Nob. Are we going for it or are we not? It's yes or no.

N: Okay, if you put it like that, what's your idea?

R: It's this! Listen, we collect ideas, patents and we sieve through them. We decide what could be produced, and sold. We contact a potential manufacturer or supplier. We give them the specifications and they produce it. Isn't that brilliant? Nobby, are you listening? Isn't that brilliant?

N: *(Dog barking)* At the minute I'm fighting with this animal under the table.

R: Disgusting, animals under tables in eating places! As I was saying, shall we go for it? *(Dog barking)*.

N: Let's drink a bottle of good red wine. Then we can really sort out the possibilities.

R: I knew you'd go for it.

(William, the owner of the pub arrives.)

W: Pardon me for interrupting gentlemen, I'm afraid I have to cash up now. We're closing.

R: What's that? Closing hours in Germany?

W: I think it's better for you two in any case.

N: If we might just finish our conversation ... and a bottle of Burgundy. ... Come on, you won't regret it. *(William leaves and comes back with a half bottle)*. To return to our project, we've got to build our team. Who can we work with? Good people are difficult to find.

R: You're right there! Let's take some people from my language services office. What about Ortrud Gram? Not much sense of humour but solid. She could manage things.

N: Hmm, she plods forward, step by step. Okay.

R: And from our translation department Annette Säuli?

N: Isn't she a bit impulsive?

R: She is but she gets things done. You only have to know how to handle her.

N: Do you know?

R: Norbert! Are we being positive or are we beaten before we even begin?

N: Okay! Okay!

R: I suggest Amy and Bryan as employees to implement the practical side. What do you say to all this?

N: Isn't Amy a bit naive? And Bryan likes a drop of beer, doesn't he?

R: Rubbish, Norbert! And what about you? You're no better!

N: You might be right. Actually, I'm not sure I'm in full control of my faculties after all this wine.

R: That's great! That's how business is really done, in the real world, Nob. Great to have you with me on this. Put it there!

(Bossybitch stretches his hand out and grasps Kleinstück's. Sound of two hands hitting each other.)

(V) Vocabulary to help you with the text

beat, beat, beaten	schlagen, schlug, geschlagen
bossy	herrisch, diktatorisch
Burgundy	Burgunder (Rotwein)
cash up	abkassieren
desperate	verzweifelt
disgusting	abscheulich
enemy	Feind
facilities	hier: Möglichkeiten
found a company	eine Firma gründen
go for it	es anpacken
in addition to	zusätzlich zu
interrupt	unterbrechen
keep on track	bei der Sache bleiben
major	wichtig, größer, bedeutend
once upon a time	es war einmal
plod forward	sich durchkämpfen
potential manufacturer	möglicher Hersteller, Produzent
sieve through	aussieben
sort out the possibilities	die Möglichkeiten sichten

specifications	Spezifikationen
step by step	Schritt für Schritt
subject	Thema, Gegenstand
supplier	Lieferant

B Task 1: Word watch

Back to our friends. Let's look at the language of their meeting.

1) How do they interrupt each other? (4 functions)

2) How do they refuse to be interrupted? (2 functions)

3) How do they go on after being interrupted? (3 functions)

(solutions see page 20)

B Task 2: Brain test

You've read the text (and listened to it if you have the CD or the cassette). Now let's see how good your memory is. Sometimes more than one answer might be correct.

1) What is Ron Bossybitch's great idea?

a Buying patents and manufacturing the article

b Buying patents and selling them to manufacturers

c Being creative, inventing things and having them patented

2) Why are they thinking of founding a company?

a Because they need money.

b Because they hate their jobs and want to give them up.

c Because they are unemployed.

3) Why are they thinking of investing time and money in patents?

a Ron thinks they are creative and inventive.

b They want to find out what it's like in the real world.

c They know people in various patent departments.

(solutions in the appendix)

Back to Task 1 – Here's the result of our word-watching

1) How they interrupt each other:

Hold on!

If I could break in a minute.

Could I just interrupt you a moment?

Pardon me for interrupting, ladies and gentlemen, ...

2) How they refuse to be interrupted:

If we might just finish our conversation.

Please let me finish my sentence.

3) How they go on after being interrupted:

As I was saying, shall we go for it?

To return to my subject ...

To go back to what I was saying ...

B Task 3: Match work

Match the numbers against the right letters. No problem for you!

	speech		**function**
1)	Perhaps I could return to your question later on.	**a**	interrupting
2)	Coming back to what I was trying to explain ...	**b**	resuming
3)	Excuse me, could I just break in a moment here?	**c**	refusal to be interrupted

B Task 4: Patch work

coming		saying		might		
	interrupt		finish		subject	
break in		sentence		return		

Try to fit the patches into the sentences below.

Could I just .... you a moment?

If we .... just .... our conversation.

Please let me finish my ....

As I was .... , shall we go for it?

To return to my .... , ...

Perhaps I could .... to your question later on ...

.... back to what I was trying to explain ...

Excuse me, could I just .... a moment here?

B Task 5: Form and Function

Tick off the most formal function, underline the least formal function.

- Hold on!
- If I may just interrupt you a moment,
- If I can just break in a minute.
- Could I just interrupt you a moment?

L Language box: Five degrees of politeness

1) A question is less direct than a statement. **2)** *"Could I ... ?"* is less direct than *"Can I ... ?"* **3)** *"May I ... ?"* is less direct than *"Could I ...?"* **4)** *"If I might ... ?"* is a very polite form of introducing your interruption. **5)** You're most polite if you soften your interruption beginning with *"I beg your pardon"*, *"Excuse me"* or *"Sorry"*.

B Task 6: Mind your Manners

Excuse me for interrupting: Transform these functions to the next higher degree of politeness.

Can I just break in a moment here? ....

If I may just say a few words about ....

If I could just come in here ....

If I may just go back to the point I was making ....

(F) Why meetings *fail*

(F) Why meetings *fail*	fehlschlagen
Meetings fail when the participants cannot or do not want to communicate. There are three big problems that most *participants* have with communication. Know them and avoid them.	Teilnehmer
1. Wrong *attitudes*	Einstellungen
Participants talk to *impress* the audience.	beeindrucken
They don't talk to each other or are not understood because they are no longer interested in each other.	
They try *to trip* their partners *up* instead of trying to strike a compromise.	reinlegen
They talk in order to *convince* and to *persuade* those who listen.	überzeugen/ überreden
2. *Inability* to listen	Unfähigkeit
They do not listen because they are *flooded* with information.	überflutet
They cannot *pay attention* because they are busy thinking about what they are going to say next.	aufpassen
They pay more attention to those speakers they agree with.	
3. Misunderstandings	
They do not speak the same language. The word 'compromise', for example, has a negative meaning in *Farsi*.	Persisch
They *misinterpret* body language.	falsch auslegen
Even if they speak the same language they misinterpret the meaning of words.	
That reminds me of a joke: A lady bought a bath and was leaving the shop when the shop assistant called: "Do you need *a plug*?" – "Why?" asked the lady. "Is it electric?"	Stöpsel, (elektrischer) Stecker

Some ideas have been taken from Fisher and Ury *Getting to Yes*. Penguin Books

The kick-off meeting

CONTENTS

Our story: The kick-off meeting
Focus: How to chair a meeting
Language box: Degrees of politeness
Brain work: We'll practise speech functions you will hear used by the chairperson
Follow-up: More reasons why meetings fail

Time for a smile

At the company board meeting[1] the chairman rose[2] to make a speech. "Who has been carrying on with[3] my secretary?" he asked. There was a long silence. No reply[4].

"Alright then," said the chairman, "let's put it this way: Who has not been carrying on with my secretary?" The youngest manager rose: "Me, sir."

"Well", said the Chairman, "then you are the only man who can sack[5] her."

1 Vorstandssitzung 2 rise, rose, risen: sich erheben 3 ein Verhältnis haben mit 4 Antwort 5 feuern, entlassen

The kick-off meeting

The following day Norbert Kleinstück (we'll call him Nob) and Ronny Bossybitch meet at the big sports ground for a jog (both puffing and blowing).

N: We're very productive when we meet in restaurants. That's where we get our best ideas. By the way, what did we finally decide?
R: In the end we said we would go ahead with establishing a company to sell ideas and patents to potential manufacturers.
N: Did we? ... I remember now. We should think of a name then. What about ICS, Invention Consultant Services?
R: Not bad at all. I've contacted our future employees and I've called a meeting for the day after tomorrow.
N: You were quick as usual.
R: Time is money. And time is short, so let's prepare the meeting.

The time: Friday, afternoon. The place: the office of PELC, Personal Executive Language Consultants. Attendees: Norbert Kleinstück (N), Ronald Bossybitch (R), Bryan Hemmung (B), Amy Fenando (A), Ortrud Gram (O), all language teachers and all a bit tired of teaching.

(Sounds of traffic on the street)
R: Damn rush hour! Could you close that window, Bryan? It's too loud. *(Bang)* Now, that's better. Well, we all know each other so I won't waste time with formalities. Let's get down to business, shall we?
B: Good idea! The quicker we start, the quicker it's over and we can go out for a couple of pints in the town.
N: Now just a minute, Bryan, we've come here to talk about a serious theme. That's not the right attitude.
R: Okay, you two. Now let's stop arguing. Perhaps we should do it formally after all. Ladies and Gentlemen, I declare the meeting open. I'll chair the meeting. Ortrud, could you take the minutes of the meeting? Now to the reason for my calling this meeting. Norbert Kleinstück and myself have decided to found a company and we'd like you to be a part of it. We know you and we know your skills.
O: Well, that's very interesting but what do we all do?

B: I think a better question would be to ask what the company would do, Ortrud. Perhaps we'll all be selling Norbert's and Ronny's boring books or something like that.

A: But I'm already doing that. I ...

R: Just a minute, Amy. Bryan was making a joke. At least he was trying to. *(Phone rings)*

R: I'll answer that. Guten Tag, Bossybitch. ... Ja, ... ah ja! ... Herzlichen Dank. Auf Wiederhören.

B: Very fluent, as always, Ron.

R: Well, my dear friends, that was the Dutch Bank. You'll all be pleased to know that Norbert and I have a meeting with them next week to present our idea, but in principle they're interested in giving us a start-up loan.

N: *(clapping)* Well, that's good news at least. But back to our meeting. I think you all received a copy of our plan. Ron distributed them yesterday.

A: Sorry, I haven't seen anything.

O: Nor have I.

N: Ron, what's gone wrong? Typical, absolutely typical! That's so amateur. We'll never succeed!

R: Now calm down, Nob. Everything's under control. There must have been a breakdown in communication. Okay, the purpose of today's meeting is to describe the project ...

B: Then why don't you describe it?

R: Okay, okay. It's simple. We receive suggestions, ideas, patents for inventions. We check them. We approach potential manufacturers and marketing people.

B: Brilliant! But who's going to do all this? Who's qualified and experienced enough?

O: If I could break in here. I have complete confidence in Ron and Norbert to manage that. But what will our functions be?

R: That's my Ortrud! Practical as usual! Functions are as follows: Ortrud, you're office manager, Annette, who didn't have time to come as usual, is responsible for documentation, Amy and Bryan, you two are company reps. You go to companies and present our ideas and products, as required.

B: Look, I've got no experience with all this.
N: Bryan, we've got complete confidence in you.
B: Well, thank you for that at least. But what are you two going to do?
N: My dear Bryan, we take the whole financial risks.
R: And we'll find projects and select the best and decide what should be offered. And now I'd like to draw this meeting to a close. Think about what we've said. I hope you're all with us. Good, now a glass of champagne to celebrate. *(Pop of cork)*

(V) Vocabulary to help you with the text

list	auflisten
apply for a loan	einen Kredit beantragen
approach someone	an jemanden herantreten
argue	streiten, argumentieren
attitude	Einstellung, Haltung
check	prüfen
declare a meeting open/closed	eine Besprechung für eröffnet / für geschlossen erklären
establish a company	eine Firma gründen
experience	Erfahrung
have complete confidence in someone	volles Vertrauen in jemanden haben
invention	Erfindung
item one on the agenda	Punkt eins der Tagesordnung
pint; a couple of ~s	ein paar Glas Bier
receive	erhalten
reps (representatives)	Vertreter
require	erfordern, benötigen
select	auswählen
skills	Fähigkeiten
stage; at this ~	zu diesem Zeitpunkt
start-up loan	Anfangs-, Anschubkredit
stick to the subject	beim Thema bleiben
suggestion	Vorschlag
take the minutes	das Protokoll führen

B Task 1: Word watch

Let's have a look at some of the speech functions used at meetings:

1) How does Ron deal with the formalities of meetings such as opening, minutes, chairing, introductions? (4 functions)

2) With five functions he announces the reason for their meeting. Which?

3) How does he end the meeting? (3 functions)

Listen or read again and find the functions **(see page 28).**

B Task 2: Brain test

You've read the text and/or listened to it. Now let's see how good your memory is. Sometimes more than one answer might be correct.

1) Why do the future employees of the Inventions Consultant Services know each other?

a They have met in pubs before.
b They are teachers working with PELC.
c They have read Ron's advertisement in the newspaper.

2) How are they going to finance the new company?

a They will put their savings together.
b They have applied for a loan.
c They don't need any money for the first phase.

3) What will the job of the company reps be?

a They will try to interest manufacturers in new ideas.
b They will visit inventors and buy their inventions.
c They will find projects and select the best.

(solutions in the appendix)

Time for a smile: Getting to know our team

Bryan Hemmung's first responsible[1] office job was cleaning the windows – on the envelopes[2].

1 verantwortlich 2 Briefumschlag

Back to Task 1 – Here's the result of our word-watching

1) How to open a meeting

I declare the meeting open.	Ich erkläre die Besprechung für eröffnet.
I'll chair the meeting.	Ich führe den Vorsitz.
Could you take the minutes of the meeting?	Könnten Sie das Protokoll übernehmen?
I won't waste time with formalities.	Ich werde keine Zeit mit Förmlichkeiten verschwenden.

2) How to announce the purpose of a meeting

I've called a meeting to ...	Ich habe die Sitzung anberaumt, um zu ...
Now, the reason for calling this meeting ...	Der Grund, warum ich zu dieser Besprechung eingeladen habe ...
The purpose of today's meeting is ...	Der Zweck der heutigen Konferenz ist ...
We've come here to talk about a serious theme.	Wir sind hierher gekommen, um über ein ernstes Thema zu reden.
You'll all be pleased to know that ...	Sie werden alle erfreut sein, zu erfahren, daß ...

3) How to end a meeting

I'd like to draw this meeting to a close.	Ich würde diese Besprechung nun gerne beenden.
Let's call it a day.	Feierabend für heute.
A glass of champagne to celebrate.	Stoßen wir zur Feier mit einem Glas Champagner an.

Time for a smile: Getting to know our team

Amy Fernando started her career as a proofreader[1] for a skywriting[2] company.

Annette Säuli has been on a diet[3] for weeks. Now she is so thin that every time she goes for a walk in the park, dogs try to bury[4] her.

1 Korrekturleser 2 skywriter: Himmelsschreiber 3 Diät 4 vergraben

B Task 3: Match work

Just do it! Match the numbers against the right letters.

	speech		function
1)	As you can see from the agenda ...	a	opening a meeting
2)	Right, shall we get started?	b	announcing the purpose
3)	I'd like to call it a day now.	c	keeping up discipline
4)	That's not the right attitude.	d	closing a meeting

B Task 4: Patch work

objective		shall we?		calling
	purpose		declare	
agenda		draw		closed
	discuss		minutes	

And now try to fit the patches into these sentences.

I .... the meeting open.

Has everyone received a copy of the .... ?

Bryan has volunteered to keep the ....

The .... of this meeting is to establish a new company.

The .... of today's meeting is ...

Now to the reason for my .... this meeting.

Let's get down to business, ... ?

Is there anything else to .... ?

I'd like to .... this meeting to a close.

I declare the meeting........................ . Thank-you, Ladies and Gentlemen!

B Task 5: Form and function

Ron was trying to discipline the participants of the first meeting. Tick off the softest, least harsh function.

- Look, Amy, couldn't we discuss that later and take item one now?
- Look, Amy, I'm afraid you're moving too far away from the subject.
- Could you stick to the subject, please?

L Language box: Degrees of politeness

1) As you know from the first chapter, questions are less direct than statements. Sometimes negative adjectives have to be changed into positive adjectives (impossible → possible)
2) Would (würde, wäre) is often used to soften a negative statement that might be unpleasant to partners.
3) In many cases you can combine 1 and 2. Let's try it.

B Task 6: Mind your manners

Transform these functions to the next higher degree of politeness

That is impossible.	Is that ....?
That is unacceptable.	....
Is that possible?	....
I'm afraid that is impossible.	....
I couldn't agree.	....

Time for a smile: Getting to know our team

"There are two sides to every question," said Ronny Bossybitch at the first meeting: "my side and the wrong side. And don't say 'yes' until I've finished."

(F) The Advertisement

Time is money. And time was short. The next step was to put an advert in the newspaper. Ronny Bossybitch was quick as usual. The following advert appeared in four British and two German newspapers. "Why British newspapers?" you might ask. Well, Ronny has unlimited confidence[1] in the ingenuity[2] of God's own people. Haven't all the really important things like knickerbockers, golf or boxing been invented by the English? Here's the advert:

Invention is mother of Prosperity[3]

You are creative?
You have brilliant ideas?
You know how to make this world
a better place to live in
– but nobody is interested?

Well, we are!

Contact ICS Ltd.
(Invention Consultant Services)
32196 Hollerberg
Krumme Gasse 3

Time for a smile: First inventions

Only four days later the first brain children of Anglo-Saxon ingenuity arrived at ICS Ltd.:

Farmer Smith from York offered his pocket size "cowculator".
A certain Dr. Twostone sent a drawing of his "Do-it-your-self kit for brain surgery".
And Bryan Hemmung brought his small electric window cleaner for window envelopes.

1 unbegrenztes Vertrauen 2 Erfindungsgabe 3 Wohlstand

(F) More *reasons* why meetings fail – Nob's notes

Gründe

Well, Ron and Nob have found their team. However, was it a good meeting? Wouldn't tired teachers do anything to get away from the *boredom* of teaching? Let's have a look at Nob's notes.

Langeweile

Disruptions

Störungen

Problem: The meeting was interrupted by a phone call.
Solution: In future switch on the *answering machine*.
Problem: We had to close the windows because of the noise. The room got too hot and very *stuffy* because of Bryan's smoking.
Solution: Choose another time of the day. No smoking!

Anrufbeantworter
stickig

Wrong time
Problem: The atmosphere could have been better.
Solution: *Further* meetings not on a Friday afternoon when people are tired and look forward to their weekend.

weitere

***Insufficient* preparation**

unzureichend

Problem: Colleagues were not prepared; they didn't know the purpose of the meeting. Annette was not able to *make it.*
Solution: *Distribution* of agenda a week in advance, to make sure members arrive with proposals.

kommen
Verteilung

***Lack* of motivation**

Mangel

Problem: Team was not as *enthusiastic* about the project as we had expected.
Solution: *Build common ground* ("we're all looking for something more interesting than teaching, aren't we?"). Ask them what they would prefer, instead of *assigning tasks* in a 'bossybitchy' way.

begeistert
Gemeinsamkeiten aufzeigen, Aufgaben zuweisen

Presenting Invention Consultant Services Ltd.

CONTENTS

Time for a smile: To fire with enthusiasm

In the next episode you will meet Dr. Hill, one of Ron's students of English and general manager of the Dutch Bank – a boss who is always right. Once, he opened up a meeting by announcing[1]:
"Ladies and gentlemen, the purpose[2] of this meeting is to fire you with enthusiasm[3]. If it doesn't work I'm going to fire[4] you – with enthusiasm."

1 ankündigen 2 Zweck 3 Begeisterung in jemandem entfachen 4 entlassen

Presenting ICS Ltd.

R: So tomorrow we'll be at the bank to make our presentation. We should try to prepare it in a professional way.

N: Right, I'll prepare some foils with a flowchart.

R: Yes, I guess it'll be a formal meeting.

At the bank. Norbert Kleinstück (N), Ronald Bossybitch (R), Dr. Hill, general manager (H), Dr. Maier (M), Frau Fünkner (F)

(Church bells ring for 10 a.m. Norbert and Ronald knock at the door of the manager's office)

Voice: Come in. Ah, Mr Bossybitch and his partner, Mr Kleinstück. Gentlemen, may I introduce you to Dr. Maier, head of investment, Mr Köbler, chief accountant and responsible for your accounts, and myself, the general manager, Dr. Hill.

N&R: How do you do, gentlemen?

H: Now we've met here to hear something about your ideas on founding a company. You'd like our support in this undertaking.

N: Yes, gentelmen. The subject of our meeting today is to give you a general idea about our strategy and targets. To make the whole thing easier we've brought our portable OHP with us.

M: Very professional, but actually we're more concerned with what you've got on your OHP foils.

R: Of course, of course. Mr Kleinstück will come to that in a moment. Do you have a flip-chart?

H: It can be arranged *(presses intercom, buzzing noise)*. Miss Fünkner, could you bring in a flip-chart, please?

F: A flip-chart, sir?

H: Yes, a flip-chart. Two legs, an oversized writing-pad of white paper – people write on it, you know!

F: Oh yes, a flip-chart on two legs, sir. But we don't have anything like that.

H: We must have! Try the training department. Have it here in five minutes. Good bye!!

N: Oh dear! Well, I'd like to begin my presentation by giving you an overview of the project. I'll be developing the three major parts of our project. To begin with, this flowchart represents our original idea to ...

(knocking on the surface of a desk)

H: Gentlemen, gentlemen! First of all your foil is upside down, or at least I think it is.

N: Oops! So it is. There!

M: If you ask me it was more understandable the other way round. What are all those arrows?

H: Mr Kleinstück. What has salary structure to do with a flowchart of your project?

N: Oh, my goodness! René, we've got the numbers on the foils mixed up.

H: Gentlemen, wouldn't it be better if we took a five-minute break? Perhaps you can sort yourselves out.

(knocking at the door; Miss Fünkner comes in)

F: Dr. Hill, I'm afraid there are no flipcharts, not even on three legs!

H: My god! It seems the bank also needs five minutes to sort itself out.

(sound of door slamming; one hour later)

N: ... and so, gentlemen, that was the basic idea.

M: Okay. I think we've understood the purpose of your company. But from my point of view there is some important data missing. We need to know figures. What about your cost structure? How much are you prepared to pay for promotion?

H: And if I might interrupt, Dr. Maier, what about potential markets? Have you collected any data on how much of a thing could be sold by you or a marketing agency, for example? Have you thought about profit margins?

R: Of course, there's still a lot of work to be done. I ...

H: *(interrupting)* If I might suggest something. Why don't you two collect the missing information, put it down in a report, preferably done together with a small marketing agency, and send it to us?

M: Yes, and then we can come to a decision.

R: Oh, right. Umhh!

H: That'll be all for now, gentlemen. Good luck! Don't forget your portable OHP and this heap of foils.

(V) Vocabulary to help you with the text

account	Konto
announce	ankündigen
arrow	Pfeil
concerned, be ~ with	hier: interessiert an
decision	Entscheidung
foil	Folie
focus on	sich konzentrieren auf
from my point of view	aus meiner Sicht
head of investment	Leiter der Investitionsabteilung
introduce; ~ someone	jemanden vorstellen
overview	Überblick
portable OHP	tragbarer Overheadprojektor
potential markets	mögliche Märkte
profit margin	Gewinnspanne
promotion	Werbung; Beförderung
represent	darstellen
salary structure	Gehaltsstruktur
sheet	Bogen, Blatt
slam the door	die Tür zuschlagen
sort oneself out	sich Klarheit verschaffen,
suggest	vorschlagen, anregen
support	Unterstützung
surface	Oberfläche
target / objective	Ziel
undertaking	Unternehmen, Vorhaben

Time for a smile: Getting to know the team

This is Ronald Bossybitch's favourite opening for presentations: "After such a hearty reception[1] I can hardly[2] wait to hear myself speak."

1 herzlicher Empfang 2 kaum

B Task 1: Word watch

Back to our friends. Let's look at the language of their meeting:

1) In the dialogue the purpose of the presentation was announced twice. Find the functions. (3)
2) How does Nob begin his presentation? (1)
3) And how does he structure his presentation? (2)
4) Twice in the dialogue Dr. Hill suggests something. How does he introduce his suggestions?(3)
(solutions see page 38)

B Task 2: Brain test

Remember: sometimes more than one solution can be right.

1) Why does Ronald Bossybitchy need a flip-chart?
a He needs it in case the OHP does not work.
b The text does not say why.
c He has prepared the salary structure on one chart.

2) What should Nob's first foil illustrate?
a The original idea of ICS Ltd.
b The salary structure of the future company
c The costs of promotion

3) What will Nob's and Ron's next step be?
a Next time they will prepare fifty OHP sheets.
b They will collect the missing information about potential markets, cost structure, promotion etc.
c They will send a written report to the bank.

(solutions in the appendix)

Time for a smile: Inventions ICS did not accept

One inventor from Britain designed[1] the all-metal pinwall.
And a German invented the Tipp-Ex[2] for computer screens.[3]

1 entwerfen 2 Tipp-Ex in English: liquid paper 3 Bildschirm

Back to Task 1 – Here's the result of our word-watching plus a few additional speech functions

Step 1: Announce the purpose of the presentation
Now we've met here to hear something about your ideas on ...
The subject of our presentation today is to ...
In my presentation I'm going to explain our new project.

Step 2: Give an overview
I'd like to begin my presentation by giving you an overview of the project.
This morning I'd like to look back at the past fiscal year.
In my presentation I will try to give you a summary of the development of our company's activities in Asia.

Step 3: Explain the structure
I'll be developing the three major parts of our project.
To begin with, let me say ...
My presentation will be in three main parts.
Firstly, I'd like to ... Secondly, we can ... And I'll finish with ...

This is how Dr. Hill introduces his suggestions
Wouldn't it be better if we took a five-minute break?
If I might suggest something.
Why don't you two collect the missing information ...?

B Task 3: Match work (1)

Match the numbers against the right letters.

speech	function
1) Let me start with ... Then I'll ...	**a** announcing the purpose
2) The objective of this presentation is to ...	**b** giving an overview
3) There are three aspects I'd like to focus upon.	**c** explaining the structure

B Task 4: Patch work

summary		main parts		major parts
	explaining		overview	
subject		begin with		focus upon
	suggest		look back	

Now use your brain and fit the patches in.

The .... of our meeting today is to ....

In my presentation I'll be .... our new project.

I'll begin my presentation by giving you an .... of the project.

This morning I'd like to .... at the past fiscal year.

I'm trying to give you a .... of our company's activities.

I'll be developing the three .... of our project.

To ...., I'd like to show you what our robot can do.

My presentation will be in three ....

There are three aspects I'd like to ....

If I might .... something. Wouldn't it be better if we took a break?

B Task 5 : Match work (2)

Match the numbers against the right letters.

speech	**function**
1) I'd like to conclude by stating ...	**a** giving an overview
2) Let's now turn to the problem of ...	**b** introducing first part
3) Let's consider the options.	**c** introducing second part
4) To begin with, let me say ...	**d** looking at alternatives
5) I'll be developing the three major parts of our project.	**e** announcing end

(L) Language box: How to create emphasis (Nachdruck)

In the dialogue Mr Hill says: "We need to know figures". There are two ways of putting more stress on a word.

First type: Start with w*hat* and emphasise the object.
What we need to know are *figures*.

Second type: Start with *It is/was (+ that) ...*
Dr. Hill wanted to know the costs of promotion.
It was the costs of promotion *(that)* Dr. Hill wanted to know.

(B) Task 6 (a difficult one): Emphasis

Now it's your turn. Emphasise the parts of the sentences in italics.

Type 1: Use *What*

In my presentation today I'm going to explain *our new project*.
I'm trying to give you a summary of our *firm's activities*.
I'll begin my presentation by giving you an *overview* of the project.

Type 2: Use *It is/was (+ that) ...*

We need a *flipchart*, Mrs Fünkner.
We will have to consult *an agency*.
They want *a full report* on the project.

(B) Task 7: Word power

Find the neighbour. Which functions have almost the same meaning?

Let's go through the possibilities / My presentation will be in three main parts / In conclusion, I'd like to say ... / Let me start with ... / The next question I would like to focus on is ...

I'll be developing the three major parts of our project ....
To begin with, let me say ....
Let's turn now to the problem of ....
Let's consider the options ....
I'd like to conclude by stating ....

(F) What went wrong?

Do you remember Nob's *desperate moan*: "Oh, my goodness! Ronny, we've got the numbers wrong on the foils." If you get your audio-visual *aids* wrong the result can vary from mild confusion to catastrophe and *humiliation*. There are a few *lessons* to be learnt from Dr. Hill's and Dr. Maier's comments.

verzweifelt; Seufzer
Hilfsmittel
Demütigung
Lehre

Keep it simple

"Gentlemen!", said Dr. Hill, "first of all, your foil is *upside down*, or at least I think it is." And Dr. Maier's comment: "If you ask me it was more understandable the other way round." So *appeal* to the imagination, not to the intellect; use pictures instead of words, *figures* and abstract symbols.

verkehrt herum
appellieren
Zahlen

Don't overload: The Magic Seven

"What are all those *arrows*?" asked Dr. Maier. Obviously there were too many arrows and other graphics on the sheet. Don't put more words or graphics on a foil than you would on a T-shirt. By the way, words are not *visuals*. If you have to use words keep to the number seven. Don't put more than seven lines (plus minus two) on the sheet; each line should have between seven and two times seven *syllables*. On the next page you will find positive and negative examples.

Pfeile
bildhafte Elemente
Silben

Not more foils than fingers

"Don't forget your portable OHP and this heap of foils." *remarked* Dr. Hill cynically. Don't use more foils than you have fingers. Seven (plus/minus two) is a *reasonable* number. And you should not speak more than seven minutes about one *transparency*. With seven foils your presentation will last about 45 minutes – that's the limit.

bemerken
vernünftig
Folie

(F) Visuals instead of words

Don't

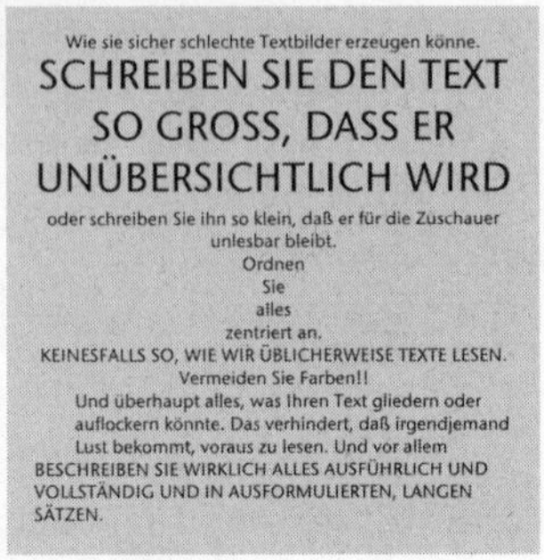

Do

Adapted from Emil Hierhold *Sicher präsentieren – wirksamer vortragen*. Verlag Carl Ueberreuter. 3. Auflage. Wien 1990

Finding the customer

CONTENTS

Our story: Finding the customer
Focus: Finding out what people think
Brain work: Asking for opinion – expressing opinion
Language box: Degrees of politeness: avoiding negative adjectives

Time for a smile: Replies to the advert

Dear Mr Bossybitch,

I've invented a wonderful new insecticide. You spray it on your plants and it promptly kills them so that the insects will then starve to death[1].

Yours sincerely
Tom Jetstream

Dear Mr Bossybitch,

I'd like you to market my new Red Indian Toaster. Before the toast pops up[2] it sends up smoke signals.

Yours faithfully
Wyatt Churp

1 verhungern 2 hochspringen, herausspringen

Finding the customer

(Bossybitch dials Kleinstück's number; telephone ringing)

R: *(to himself)* Come on, come on! Where are you? Ah, there you are, Nob. Why do you always take so long to get to the phone?

N: It's my new ISDN system. It doesn't seem to work properly.

R: Hmm! Listen, I've had a letter from the Dutch Bank. Our efforts have paid off. They're granting us start-up capital of DM 150 000.

N: Great! That'll cover costs till we find a cash-cow.

R: Cash-cow? You've been doing some reading.

N: Just brushing up on my business principles.

R: Very impressive! Keep brushing. See you at the meeting this afternoon.

At the office. Ortrud Gram (O), Amy Fernando (A), Bryan Hemmung (B), Norbert Kleinstück (N), Ronald Bossybitch (R) and a postman (P)

N: *(banging on the desk)* Now ladies and gentlemen, I'd like to begin by thanking you all for coming here today.

B: Ha, ha, ha. Well, we had no choice. Ronald told us we should be here by four o'clock. So here we are!

N: Good! Well, thank-you anyway. Our topic today deals with marketing. We'd like suggestions from your side on how we can get the inventions to our potential customers. Ron, could you start us off?

R: Well, it's quite clear that the first thing we have to do is contact a small but well-established advertising agency as soon as possible.

A: You mean a marketing firm, don't you Ron?

R: Actually, Amy, we've already had some market research done on this matter.

B: Just a minute! You didn't mention anything about that.

N: It was mentioned. We told you last Saturday.

R: Remember Saturday, Bryan? It normally comes after Friday for most people. Not in your case. When you go out celebrating in the town on Friday, Saturday never comes for you.

B: Now then, Ronald. Don't start getting bossy!

R: If we could come back to the point. The result of the market research was that there is a potential market and that industry is still looking for certain innovations. The bank needed the information.

O: And was this information acceptable to them?

N: Indeed it was, wasn't it Ron?

R: Well, they seemed to swallow it. Now, if we could return to the issue in hand. How can we get the inventions to our potential customers. I'm quite sure that at this stage we need to use an advertising agency to help us to place our inventions. They're the experts regarding where to put what. What do you think of it, Amy?

A: If you ask me ..., ... well, I 'm afraid that an agency would be too expensive. ... What about putting adverts in the local press for each invention?

B: I think it'll require more than local adverts, Amy. As I see it we'll need a complete advertising campaign, won't we?

O: If I could turn to another subject. Has anybody thought about the legal aspects? I'd like to hear your views on that. They are certainly many rules and regulations concerning patents here in Germany.

B: You can say that again! They need a law for everything here. Eveything's over-organised.

R: Well, thank-you for your usual contribution, Bryan. Now to return to our problem ...

(doorbell rings)

O: Just a moment. I'll get that.

P: Päckchen für Konsul Tant aus England. Sind Sie das?

O: Oh, a parcel for you, Ronald. Could you come here and sign for it? They're always arriving at the wrong time.

R: Okay. Wo unterschreibe ich?

P: Hier.

N: This could be a reaction to our advert. The first invention.

(Ron signs, and the postman gives him a black look)

P: Entschuldigung! Hier muß Konsul Tant unterschreiben und nicht Sie. Das ist Vorschrift.

O: Hier gibt es keinen Konsul Tant. Consultant, das ist Teil des Firmennamens. Herr Bossybitch ist der Firmeninhaber.

P: Das geht nicht! Kein Konsul Tant, kein Paket.

B: I think I can hear something ticking inside. Da tickt etwas im Paket. Just wait a minute. ... Why is he running away?

O: Obviously they've both got a tick – the parcel and the postman.

(V) Vocabulary to help you with the text

advertising agency	Werbeagentur
at this stage	zu diesem Zeitpunkt
black look; give someone a ~ ~	jemanden böse anblicken
brush up	aufpolieren
cash-cow	Melkkuh, Goldesel
certain	gewiß, sicher
choice	(Aus-)Wahl
contribution	Beitrag
cover costs	Kosten abdecken
effort	Anstrengung, Mühe
grant someone a loan	jemandem einen Kredit gewähren
impressive	eindrucksvoll
law	Gesetz
legal aspects	juristische Aspekte
opinion	Meinung
pay off	lohnen
potential customer	möglicher Kunde
regarding	betreffend
require	erfordern, verlangen
rule	Regel, Vorschrift
sign	unterschreiben
swallow	schlucken
view	Ansicht

Time for a smile: Replies to the advert

ICS did not accept the new map of the Sahara. It was a sheet of sandpaper.

One inventor sent his global toaster. It works either on AC or DC[1], but not with bread. And it has two settings[2]: too soon or too late.

1 AC: Wechselstrom, DC: Gleichstrom 2 Einstellung

B Task 1: Word watch

Don't be shy, find the functions:

1) How do Ron, Nob and Ortrud ask for the other's opinions? (4)
2) How are their opinions introduced? (4)
3) How do they come back to or lead away from a point? (4)
(solutions see page 48)

B Task 2: Brain test

Sometimes more than one answer is correct.

1) When did this meeting take place?
- **a** after they had found an advertising and a marketing agency
- **b** after Dr. Hill had read the report
- **c** after they had put adverts in some newspapers

2) Why did the postman not give them the parcel?
- **a** The address was wrong.
- **b** The name of the company was wrong.
- **c** Konsul Tant lives next door.

3) Why does Ron want to use an advertising agency?
- **a** Ron thinks that he is not an expert in this field.
- **b** They don't know the German rules and regulations.
- **c** It was Dr. Hill's suggestion.

(solutions in the appendix)

B Task 3: Match work

Now here are more phrases. What are their functions?

	speech		**function**
1)	Excuse me, may I ask a question?	**a**	find out what they think
2)	Thank you for your question which leads us back to our main problem.	**b**	you say what you think
3)	Where do you stand on this issue?	**c**	someone interrupts you
4)	I think it would be fair to say ...	**d**	come back to your point

Back to Task 1 – Here's the result of our word-watching

1) How to find out what they think

What do you think of it, Amy?
We'd like suggestions from your side on the project.
I'd like to hear your views on that.
Has anybody thought about the legal aspects?

2) How to say what you think (I/my are stressed)

I think that it'll require more than local adverts, Amy.
As *I* see it we'll need a complete advertising campaign.
If you ask *me* I 'm afraid an agency would be expensive.
It's quite clear that ...

3) Coming back to or leading away from a point

If we could come back to the point.
If we could return to the issue in hand.
To return to our problem ...
If I could turn to another subject.

B Task 4: Patch work – Fill the gap

point		turn to		leads
	stand		issue	
seems		position		views
	opinion		tend to	

Ask them what they think

I'd like to hear your .... on that.
What's your .... on consulting an advertising agency?
Where exactly do you .... on this issue?

Tell them what you think

If you ask my .... I'm afraid that would be expensive.
I .... think that we should consult an agency.
It .... to me that we should start an advertising campaign.

Return to your point

That .... us back to our main problem.
If we could come back to the ....
If I could .... another subject.
If we could return to the ....

B Task 5: Form and function

Which opinion is the strongest?

- In my opinion the product will be a flop.
- I'm quite sure that the product will be a flop.
- It appears to me that the product might be a flop.

L Language box: Degrees of politeness[1]

less polite, more direct	more polite, and less direct
statements	**questions (+ would, may etc.)**
That is too early.	Isn't that too early?
Is that too early?	Would that be too early?
Can I use your car?	Could I use your car?
May I use your car?	Might I use your car?
Sorry/excuse me, but ...	**I beg your pardon, but ...**
Excuse me, but that's wrong.	I beg your pardon, but is that right?
Sorry, but that's wrong.	I beg your pardon, but isn't that wrong?
negative adjective	**not+ (very) + positive adjective**
Friday is incovenient.	Friday is not very convenient.
Friday is not very convenient.	Friday wouldn't be very convenient.
Friday wouldn't be very convenient.	I'm afraid Friday wouldn't be very convenient.

1 See also chapter 1 and 2

B Task 6: Mind your manners – Revision exercise

Now it's your turn. Transform these functions to the next higher degree of politeness.

I'll call you back later. ....

Can I ask you a question? ....

That's a negative attitude. ....

Excuse me, but I think these figures are wrong. ....

B Task 7: What went wrong?

The way Bossybitch handled the last meeting was again far from perfect. Do you remember the main mistakes? If not, maybe these two quotations will help you. You'll find our answer in the key.

1.

N: *(banging the desk)* Now ladies and gentlemen, I'd like to begin by thanking you all for coming here today.

B: Ha, ha, ha. Well, we had no choice. Ronald told us we should be here by four o'clock. So here we are!

2.

R: Actually, Amy, we've already had some market research done on this matter.

B: Just a minute! You didn't mention anything about that.

N: It was mentioned. We told you at the last meeting.

Time for a smile: A reply to the advert (page 31)

"I don't like your advert at all. I used to be a bookbinder in a large publishing house. They invented a robot that could do everything I did, and better. But the most depressing thing is that my wife went out and bought one."

P.P.P – The Personal Parking Protector

CONTENTS

Our story: P.P.P. – The Personal Parking Protector
Focus: The language of presentation
Brain Work: Phrases used by presenters
Language box: Degrees of flexibility and directness and other useful speech functions
Follow-up: Mr Otto's flipchart sheets

Time for a smile: Explosive invention

After an exciting[1] day at the R&D department inventor Fred Lobel comes home and tells his wife:
"This morning we finished all the experiments with the new explosive[2] that I invented for the company. Let's go on holiday."
"And after the holiday, what are you going to invent next for the company?"
Fred was astonished: "Which company?"

1 aufregend 2 Sprengstoff

P.P.P. – The Personal Parking Protector

(Ronald's telephone rings)

R: Hello, Bossybitch speaking. Can I help you?

N: Hi, it's me, Nob. How are things?

R: Don't even ask! Anything new?

N: There is indeed. There's an inventor, a certain Mr Otto, coming to see us to make a presentation. Maybe this is the big fish.

R: Or the one that got away. Okay, let's fix Wednesday. Can you make the arrangements?

Wednesday, 12th June, at the office. Norbert Kleinstück (N), Ronald Bossybitch (R), Amy Fernando (A), Bryan Hemmung (B), Ortrud Gram (O), the inventor, Mr Otto (I)

(Many loud voices at the same time. Banging on the desk).

R: Ladies and Gentlemen, and you as well, Bryan, come to order, please. The reason for our gathering today is that we have the honour of being addressed by Mr H. Otto from Darmstadt on the theme of his P.P.P.

B: You didn't by any chance invent an engine in the past, did you?

I: No, unfortunately that was only my namesake. Gentlemen, may I say that I'm very happy to be here. I'm also glad to have the chance to speak to you in English since I spent three years in Britain which is, by the way, where I had this little idea, the P.P.P.

A: What does P.P.P. stand for? It sounds like my medical insurance, the Private Patients Plan.

O: No, my dear, but it is a kind of insurance. P.P.P. means Personal Parking Protector. Let me explain with the help of a flipchart and the hand-out in front of you. Here on the flipchart you see the idea: the

Sheet 1: The Problem

typical everyday situation in my home town. We park our cars, go away for ten minutes, return and cannot drive off. We are "parked in" as we tend to say. You cannot drive away. Totally frustrated you phone the police. They do not arrive. Look at the upper right-hand corner of the flipchart. There you are. There is your anger, your inability to do anything. The next stage will be a stroke or a heart attack. Do something for your health, gentlemen!

B: Splendid, splendid. I'm into all that health stuff.

N: Except at the weekends.

B: Hey, what do you mean by that below-the-belt statement? You know I'm into strengthening my body with body building.

N: Well, your arms are strong enough but that's from holding beer glasses.

B: Not to mention your "bottle of Sekt per day keeps the doctor away", Norbert.

R: *(Desk banging)* Order! Order! Now then, you two! This isn't a kindergarten! Mr Otto, please tell us more.

I: Yes gentlemen, please ...

A: *(Amy, interrupting)* Excuse me, I'm a lady.

B: Hmm. No comment!

A: I beg your pardon!

I: And I beg your pardon too, madam! I was perfectly aware that you're a lady.

A: I mean you should say "ladies and gentlemen."

I: Oh, excuse me. I am sorry! Now to my flipchart and the solution to our parking problems.
The device D prevents the blocking of your parked car. The bumper bar B is movable and can expand the length of your car. It is driven by the electrical motor M, a gear-wheel G and a tooth rack R ...
By the way, young lady, you seem to be taking notes and copying the

Sheet 2: The Solution

drawings. May I draw your attention to my handout. It's all there. Now, back to my P.P.P. and how to handle it in five steps.

(The inventor turns to the flipchart and reads out sheet three)

Now, let's look to the future, young lady, gentlemen. The next version, the P.P.P. deluxe will be equipped with a magic eye. When a car wants to park in front of you, the bumper moves out automatically.

(Applause)

B: Well, I'm really impressed, no doubt about that!

O: Are you sure, Mr Otto, that such things are legal?

I: Legal? How can it be illegal, madam? It's so simple, so brilliant!

R: Yes, we're all sure it is. Now, on behalf of the others present I'd like to thank you for your efforts. We will certainly be in touch. Thank you once again and good bye!

(Doorbell rings)

R: Ortrud, could you deal with that?

(5 minutes later)

O: I'm afraid the heavy hand of the law has intervened again. Ron, your car has been towed away.

R: What do you mean towed away?

O: The police came with a lorry, put a chain round your bumpers, pulled the car onto a lorry and drove away with your car.

Sheet 3: *How to handle the P.P.P. in five steps*

1) *Park the car at a good distance from the car in front and behind.*
2) *Move the bumper bar out to expand the length.*
3) *Adjust the distance depending on your driving experience.*
4) *Return to your car after shopping and retract the bumper to its original position.*
5) *Drive the car out of the parking lot. Well done!*

B: Well, thank you Ortrud, for the lecture in linguistics. I mean why was it towed away?

O: The police put a note on your car yesterday that the road was to be repaired on the following day. You didn't move the car so they towed it away.

R: But I was outside Germany on business! They can't do that! What's my lawyer's number? What we need is an invention to eliminate the police.

O: *(to herself)* He's so naive for somebody who's lived here so long.

(V) Vocabulary to help you with the text

adjust the distance	den Abstand regeln, anpassen
anger	Ärger
aware; be ~ of something	sich einer Sache bewußt sein
be into something	gerne haben, sehr mögen
below the belt	unter der Gürtellinie
boot	Kofferraum
bumper	Stoßstange
depending on	abhängig von
device	Gerät, Vorrichtung
doubt	Zweifel
draw attention to	die Aufmerksamkeit lenken auf
drawings	Zeichnungen
eliminate	entfernen, ausschalten
expand	erweitern, verlängern
gathering	Zusammenkunft
gear-wheel	Zahn-, Getrieberad
glad to have the chance	erfreut sein über die Gelegenheit
hand-out	Tischvorlage
have the honour of ...	die Ehre haben, zu ...
heavy hand of the law	die schwere Hand des Gesetzes
hood (AE), bonnet (BE)	Motorhaube
inability	Unfähigkeit
insurance	Versicherung
intervene	eingreifen
lecture in linguistics	Vorlesung über Linguistik
movable	beweglich
namesake	Namensvetter
on behalf of	im Namen von
order!	Ruhe!

prevent	verhindern
protector	Beschützer
retract the bumper	die Stoßstange zurückziehen
splendid	prächtig
stroke	Schlaganfall
tooth rack	Zahnstange
touch; we'll be in ~	Sie hören von uns
tow away	abschleppen
upper right-hand corner	die obere rechte Ecke

B Task 1: Word watch

Can you find the following 11 functions?

1) How does Ronald open the meeting? (1)

2) How does he keep discipline? (3)

3) How does Mr Otto begin his presentations? (2)

4) How does Mr Otto try to get the participants' attention? (2)

5) How does Ron thank Mr Otto and close the meeting? (3)

(solutions see page 58)

B Task 2: Brain test

Now let's see how good your memory is. Sometimes more than one answer is correct.

1) What is Mr Otto presenting?

a an electric motor
b an insurance plan
c part of a car

2) Where is the P.P.P. fitted?

a under the hood
b in the boot
c under the front seats

3) How does the P.P.P. help you?

a It keeps cars at a distance.

b The bumper moves out when the magic eye sees a car coming.

c It pushes the car in front of you forward if necessary.

4) Why was Ronald's car towed away?

(solution in the appendix)

B Task 3: Match work

speech	function
1) Mr Otto is going to give us a presentation of his latest invention.	a opening a meeting
2) That concludes our business for today. Thank you.	b announcing the theme
3) If we look more closely at the P.P.P., we'll notice it's magic eye.	c keeping discipline
4) I shall have to call you to order, Mr Brain.	d focusing attention
5) Right, shall we get started?	e closing the meeting

B Task 4: Patch work – words presenters use

happy		attention		proposing
	first		upper part	
present		draw		to begin with
	handout		explaining	

Now its your turn. Put the patches in the right places.

I'm glad to have the chance to .... you my P.P.P.

I'll be .... a solution to your parking problems.

.... , let me give you an overview of the P.P.P.

.... , I'd like to show you what my P.P.P. can do for you.

Second, I'll be .... how my P.P.P. works.

I'd be .... to answer any of your questions.

May I .... your attention to the the second slide?

The .... of the slide shows the P.P.P. in action.

In the .... that I'll be passing round you'll find the details.

Ladies and gentlemen, thank you for your ....

Back to Task 1 – Here's the result of our word-watching

1) How to open a meeting

The reason for our gathering today is that we have the honour of being addressed by Mr Otto from D. on the theme of his P.P.P.

2) How to keep discipline

Ladies and Gentlemen come to order, please.
Now then, you two! This is not a kindergarten!
Order! Order!

3) Starting the presentation: introduction and polite noises

Gentlemen, may I say that I'm very happy to be here.
I'm also glad to have the chance to speak to you in English since I spent three years in Britain which is, by the way, where I had this little idea, the P.P.P.

4) How to focus your audience's attention

May I draw your attention to the handout in front of you?
Please, look at the upper right-hand corner of the flipchart.

5) How to close the meeting and thank the presenter

Now, on behalf of the others present I'd like to thank you for your efforts.
Thank you once again and good bye!
We will certainly be in touch.

(L) Language box: Degrees of flexibility and directness

Gemans tend to be direct and categorical. Anglo-Saxons tend to be flexible and indirect. They restrict their statements using words like: a slight, a little, a bit (of a); a little bit; short, some etc.

more direct	**less direct**
Your prices are high.	I'm afraid, your prices are *a little* too high.
I think that *will* be a problem for us.	I think that *would* be *a bit of a problem.*
I have my doubts about this project.	I've/*might have/some*/doubts about this project.
The article has a defect.	I'm afraid, the article has/might have/a *slight* defect.

(B) Task 5: Mind your manners. Don't be too direct!

more direct	**less direct**
We need more money for the project.	I'm afraid .... more money for the project.
We have a cash-flow problem.	I'm afraid, we ....
I have reservations as to the success the P.P.P.	I have .... as to the success of the P.P.P.
I think that is dangerous.	I'm afraid .... dangerous
Send us a description of your invention.	Please send us .... invention.

More than one solution is possible.

Time for a smile

The man who can smile when a presentation goes wrong is thinking of a colleague he can blame it on[1].

1 die Schuld schieben auf

(F) Mr Otto's flipchart sheets

The verbal sheet is *a killer*

Mr Otto's third sheet is a verbal one without pictures, with nothing but words. Obviously he has *observed* the rule of the magic seven (see chapter 3). However, even if you have a slide with seven *snappy* slogans, it can be a killer. Why have a text on a slide if you repeat the words one by one? Are you going to read the words aloud, as if you wanted to teach them how to read? But what else could you do than repeat aloud word by word? And there is another problem. Your audience all listen at the same speed – the speed of your reading – but they all read at different speeds. So you *split* your audience into several groups. Mr Otto's third sheet was the weakest because it was a verbal one.

tödlich sein
beachten
schlagkräftig
spalten

The *impact* sheet is visual

An audience is able *to take in* pictures and listen at the same time to the presenter commenting on them. Mr Otto's first flipchart sheet is a visual sheet. It makes an impact on the audience. With one glance they grasp the situation (the parking problem) and react *emotionally* to it. It should be the most memorable image of your whole presentation. In our case it makes the audience *aware* of a problem that everybody has experienced. And Mr Otto is the first to have *come up with a* solution to this problem.

starker Eindruck
aufnehmen, verarbeiten
gefühlsmäßig
bewußt
aufwarten mit

Time for a smile

Ronald: Now, Amy. This isn't a kindergarten. Order! Order!
Amy: Okay, I'll have a cheese sandwich then.

To park or not to park

CONTENTS

Our story: To park or not to park
Focus: Agreeing and disagreeing; How to add new facts
Brainwork: Let's practise agreement and disagreement
Language box: Degrees of disagreement
Follow-up: Compromise – the middle-of-the-road policy

Time for a smile

We owe a lot to Thomas Alva Edison – if it wasn't for him, we'd be watching television by candlelight[1].

Milton Berle

If builders built buildings the way programmers wrote programs, then the first woodpecker[2] that came along would destroy civilisation.

Arthur Bloch

1 Kerzenlicht 2 Specht

To park or not to park

R: *(dialling)* Is that you Norbert? Hi. What did you think of the P.P.P. and that fellow?

N: Well, he was very self-confident, not at all nervous.

R: He's probably been presenting that thing for years.

N: Well, we'll discuss it tomorrow. When's the meeting?

R: Nine o'clock sharp in the office. See you then!

Ronald Bossybitch (R), Norbert Kleinstück (N), Amy Fernando (A), Bryan Hemmung (B), Ortrud Gram (O)

(Church bell sounds 'nine'. Dong, dong, dong ...)

R: Okay, let's forget the formalities.

B: Can you do that, Ronald? Wonders never cease!

R: As always, thank you, Bryan, for your support. Now, as you all know we're here to discuss the innovation or rather the invention we saw presented several days ago.

N: *(coughing)* Well, for my part of course, I'm no expert on the technology, but I thought Otto had come up with a damn good idea.

R: Yes, Norbert, I can go along with that. If this little town is typical, which it seems to be, there is a serious parking problem. This invention would certainly give us all an extra metre or two in length.

B: If I could just add something here. First I agree with you two about the practicalness of the invention. But what I would like to stress is its usefulness in helping to relax the driver. It can take the stress off him. Just like Otto said. I'd like to support this idea of taking care of one's health.

R: Good. To turn to another matter, Ortrud, what's the official situation with the patent for this device?

O: As soon as the meeting was finished last week, I telephoned a friend in a company. He has a network link-up world-wide to patents granted in this field in the last two years. Mr Otto filed a patent, fourteen months ago. He has it safely under lock and key. And there's something ...

R: Yes, yes! Until somebody or some company puts in an opposition.

B: Let's worry about that later. At the moment it's looking good.

A: Well, it's not much use to people who don't drive or who haven't got a car. Me, I ...

B: Amy, sorry for interrupting but you need to have vision. I don't have a car either, and I hate the things, but you have to imagine what might be a big hit, what will make money!

N: Yes, that's right. And if we think there is a market for it we must organise the documentation and send it to potential customers.

B: Oh, and regarding that matter, where's Annette today? She's responsible for all the brochures and documentation, isn't she?

N: Of course she is, but due to an excessive amount of work in her own company, you know, translation and documentation etc., she was unable to join us.

B: Well, that's unusual, isn't it?

A: Ronny tried to get her to come but he got his ear bitten off.

R: Well, thank you for that, Amy. Annette was otherwise indisposed.

B: I bet she was. She's always busy when it's time for a meeting.

R: I can't quite agree with you, Bryan. She's just very busy, unlike some people.

N: Sorry to interrupt your local squabbles but could we keep to the point? What should we do? Shall we put it in the hands of the advertising agency? Ron what's your feeling?

R: It looks good. Let's do it! Well, let's put it to the vote then. Those in favour raise their hands.

(Mumbling positively: Okay! Great! Ping, the sound of a desk bell which Ortrud has just hit)

O: Gentlemen, and Amy! I wish to add two sentences to the discussion to bring reality and light.

B: Oh God! The voice of doom has sounded.

O: In spite of Bryan's words it is as follows: I telephoned the Department of Transport last week. They informed me that if we try to introduce this device they will make problems for us for abusing other car drivers' rights. We will be prosecuted.

(Great grunting from the masses)

And, more important, this town council and I suppose all similar ones intend to cancel all car parking in the central areas anyway. They want to introduce parking spaces for bicycles.

R: Oh my God! That's brilliant for the future economy. Why didn't you say that before?

O: Actually, I tried to Ron, but you interrupted me.

A: Does that mean Mr Otto's invention is a non-starter?

N&R: Grr! Grrr!

(V) Vocabulary to help you with the text

abuse someone's rights	jemandes Rechte verletzen
add	hinzufügen
bet	wetten
bite, bit, bitten	beißen
cancel	streichen, absagen,
cease	enden; aufhören, einstellen
come up with an idea	eine Idee haben
device	Gerät, Vorrichtung
due to	wegen
excessive amount of work	übermäßig viel Arbeit
field; in this ~	auf diesem Gebiet
file a patent	ein Patent anmelden
for my part	was mich angeht, meinerseits
get someone to do something	jemanden dazu bringen, etwas zu tun
go along with something	mit etwas einverstanden sein
grant a patent	ein Patent erteilen
grunt	grunzen
have vision	Weitblick haben
hit (n.)	Treffer, Hit
indisposed	unpäßlich
join someone	sich jemandem anschließen
length	Länge
light (n.)	Licht
network link-up	Zugang zu einem Netzwerk
nine o'clock sharp	Punkt neun Uhr
non-starter	Versager, Niete
practicalness	die praktische Seite
put in an opposition	Widerspruch einlegen
regarding that matter	was diese Sache anbelangt

self-confident	selbstbewußt
squabble	Zank, Kabbelei
stress (v.; n.)	betonen; Betonung
suppose	annehmen, vermuten
town council	Gemeinderat
turn to	sich zuwenden
under lock and key	unter Dach und Fach
usefulness	Nützlichkeit
doom; voice of ~ has sounded	Schicksal; die Stimme des ~s hat gesprochen
what's your feeling?	wie denkst du darüber?
wonders never cease!	es gibt noch Zeichen und Wunder

B Task 1: Word watch

Find the hidden functions.

1) Find typical phrases used to chair a meeting. (6)

2) What speech functions did they use to add new arguments or to turn away from the subject? (5)

3) How did they agree and disagree? (4)

(solutions see page 66)

B Task 2: Brain test

How good is your memory? Sometimes more than one answer is correct.

1) When did Mr Otto file his patent?

a two years ago
b fourteen months ago
c several days ago

2) Why is the P.P.P. a non-starter?

a The department of transport will make problems.
b The town council will cancel car parking in the central areas.
c The patent is under lock and key.

(solutions in the appendix)

Back to Task 1 – Here's the result of our word-watching

1) How the meeting was chaired

Now, as you all know, we're here to discuss the invention we saw presented several days ago.

Let's forget the formalities.

Could we keep to the point?

Let's worry about that later. At the moment it's looking good.

Well, let's put it to the vote.

Those in favour raise their hands.

2) How to bring in new facts

I'd like to add ...

If I could just add something here.

I wish to add two sentences to the discussion ...

And, more important, they intend to cancel all car parking.

To turn to another matter ...

3) How they agreed and disagreed

I agree with you about the practicalness of the invention.

I'd like to support this idea of taking care of one's health.

I can't quite agree with you, Bryan.

Yes, Norbert, I can go along with that.

Time for a smile: More useful inventions

Mr Otto has invented another interesting machine. It does the work of 55 men. It's even got a built-in[1] strike-leader[2] .

Bryan suggested a revolutionary deaf-aid[3] : a card which the deaf person hangs across his chest[4] , with the word SHOUT![5] printed on it.

1 eingebaut 2 Streikführer 3 Hörgerät 4 Brust 5 schreien, brüllen

B Task 3: Match work

	speech		function
1)	Could you stick to the subject, please?	**a**	agreement
2)	I'd like to support this idea of ...	**b**	disagreement
3)	As well as X , there is also Y.	**c**	adding new facts
4)	Let's forget formalities.	**d**	keeping discipline
5)	How are you feeling about it, Ron?	**e**	creating atmosphere
6)	I'd like to agree. Nevertheless ...	**f**	asking for opinion

B Task 4: Patch work

disagree with		stress		opinion
	stick to		point	
go along		support		raise
	put		quite agree	

Now its your turn. Put the patches in the right places.

Well, let's .... it to the vote.

Those in favour .... their hands.

What I would like to .... is the usefulness of the device.

I .... you about the practicalness of the invention.

I'd like to .... this idea of taking care of one's health.

Could you .... the subject, please?

Could you keep to the .... Bryan?

I really can't share your .... about this project.

I can .... with your suggestion.

I can't .... with you, Bryan.

(L) Language box: Degrees of disagreement

How to announce your disagreement

Most Britons (with the exception of Ronny Bossybitch of course) are less direct than Germans. They prepare their partners for a disagreement to soften the shock. They use phrases like these:

I'm afraid ...	Leider; ich fürchte ...
Frankly, ...	Ehrlich gesagt, ...
To be honest, ...	Um ehrlich zu sein, ...
In fact, ...	Tatsächlich; eigentlich ...
With respect, ...	Bei allem Respekt, ...

How to disagree in a friendly way

You have a point there, but I'm afraid it's not as easy as you think.	Sie haben nicht ganz Unrecht, aber ich fürchte, es ist nicht so leicht, wie Sie denken.
I'd like to agree. Nevertheless I've some reservations.	Ich würde Ihnen gerne zustimmen. Trotzdem habe ich einige Bedenken.
I have some sympathy with your position, but please remember ...	Ihr Standpunkt ist mir nicht ganz fremd, aber bitte bedenken Sie ...
To a certain extent I agree with you, but I'm not totally convinced.	Ich stimme mit Ihnen bis zu einem gewissen Grad überein, bin aber nicht völlig überzeugt.

How to disagree in a neutral way

I'm afraid I can't quite agree with you.	Ich kann Ihnen leider nicht ganz zustimmen.
With respect, I see it a little differently.	Nehmen Sie es mir nicht übel, aber ich sehe dies etwas anders.
I can't help feeling that I must disagree.	Ich kann leider nicht umhin, anderer Meinung zu sein.
To be honest, I can't share your opinion.	Ehrlich gesagt, ich kann Ihre Meinung nicht teilen

Strong disagreement

To be quite frank, you're completely mistaken.	Um ganz ehrlich zu sein, Sie liegen da ganz falsch.
I totally disagree with you about that.	Ich bin da ganz anderer Meinung als Sie.
I'm sorry, but I don't agree at all about that.	Tut mir leid, aber ich bin damit überhaupt nicht einverstanden.

B Task 5: Form and function

Tick off the neutral form of disagreement.

- ▪ To put it bluntly, your arguments don't hold water.
- ▪ I'm afraid I can't see your point there.
- ▪ You seem to have a point there. All the same ...

B Task 6: Word power

Match the friendly, neutral and strong phrases of disagreement.

1) I see what you mean, although ...
2) With due respect, what you are saying is impossible.
3) I'm afraid I can't see your point there.

a We'll have to agree to differ.
b I don't disagree altogether. Still ...
c To be quite frank, you're completely mistaken.

Time for a smile

A patent application[1] will be preceded[2] by one week by a similar[3] application made by your competitor[4].

The solution to a problem changes the nature of the problem.

Arthur Bloch

1 Patentanmeldung 2 vorausgehen 3 gleich, ähnlich 4 Konkurrent

(F) Compromise – the middle-of-the-road strategy

Hard on the problem but soft on the people

One of the *goals* of a meeting is to come to an agreement or to solve problems. So don't *treat* the participants of a meeting as your *opponents*. It is dangerous to win arguments at the cost of your partners' good will. Keep the people *apart* from the problems and you can be hard on the problem while being soft on the people.

Ziele
behandeln
Gegner
getrennt von

Trust and *distrust*

Mißtrauen

Of course, you cannot always trust the people at the *negotiating table*, but you shouldn't distrust them either. If you concentrate on your interests and try to find out your partners' interests you can develop a strategy that is *independent* of trust and distrust.

Verhandlungstisch
unabhängig

Disagreement and compromise

If there is no agreement, try to find a compromise acceptable to all parties. The best way is neither to *apply pressure* nor to *yield* to pressure. However, yield to reason and common sense. Try to propose a number of *options* based on objective criteria. If you accept a compromise you can always add a condition. If you *reject* it, leave a chance for another compromise. Wise compromise is one of the basic principles and *virtues* of the British. Even the British weather is a fair compromise between *fog* and rain.

annehmbar
Druck ausüben
nachgeben
Alternativen
ablehnen
Tugenden
Nebel

How to handle a conflict

Strong disagreement is relatively rare in English. However, sometimes matters get to a point when it is best to leave. Do so quickly and politely. You might say for example:

"I'm sorry you feel so strongly about that, Ronald. I *suggest* we meet again tomorrow when we've both had some time to think things over."

vorschlagen

Bed-wetting

CONTENTS

Time for a smile: Modern technology

The Concorde travels at twice the speed of sound[1], which is fun, except that you can't hear the movie[2] until two hours after you land.

With today's technology, flying is much faster. To give you an idea of how fast we travelled: When we left we had two rabbits[3], and when we got there, we still had only two.

Bob Hope

1 Schallgeschwindigkeit 2 Film 3 Kaninchen

Bed-wetting

N: *(to himself)* Let's see. *(dials)* 27590. Hi, is that you, Ron? How are things? Don't tell me! Pity about that idea with P.P.P.

R: Yes, I thought we had something there. Better luck next time.

N: And next time is next Friday morning. We got a letter from an inventor about some household improvements. He is going to demonstrate some things to us at 10 o'clock. He says he'll arrive at 9:55 and begin at ten sharp and he doesn't need time for preparation. I'm a bit worried that something will go wrong.

R: Take it easy! You worry too much. See you on Friday.

Ronald Bossybitch (R), Norbert Kleinstück (N), Amy Fernando (A), Ortrud Gram (O), Prof. Dr. Jikon (J), Bryan Hemmung (B)

N: Ladies and gentlemen, may I open this meeting now? The reason for our coming together is to hear Professor Jokin's presentation of several improvements for the home.

J: It's ... Jikon actually. Professor Dr. ...

N: No, no I'm not a professor and I don't even have a doctorate.

J: You misunderstand. I'm the professor and my name's Jikon.

N: Oh dear, oh dear. Got myself confused again. I do beg your pardon.

J: Please don't worry! These things happen. That reminds of a joke ...

B: I'm sorry to break in, gentlemen, but we hardly have time to discuss titles. Time is money. By the way, speaking of time. Where is Annette?

R: She is sending off some advertising sheets.

B: At least she's doing some real work!

(Rustling of papers)

J: I will now begin. For my demonstration I need a tap.

A: Excuse me, did you say a tap?

B: Yes, he did, Amy. It's a sort of metal pipe with a valve. When you turn it water runs through.

O: I'm sure that Amy knows perfectly well what a tap is, Bryan. Professor Jekyll, we have a wash-basin here. If you'd like to wash your hands ...

J: My name is Jikon, actually, ... Professor Dr. Jikon.

O: Oh, I'm most awfully sorry, sir. I had no intention of hurting your feelings.

J: That's all right. We all make mistakes, don't we? Now, back to our theme. Here is a model of a room in a typical house.

B: Where? I certainly can't see anything. The model's too small.

A: Perhaps we should move our chairs in closer.

R: Ortrud, could you just shift the chairs and the tables, please?

O: It would have been more correct if the preparations had been done in advance.

J: I do apologise young lady! I do regret that I was unable to come one hour earlier. Well ... now, please look at the model. I want to present a burglar alarm to you. This invention is not my own. It was designed and patented more than eighty years ago in the United States. Have you an OHP?

O: Actually you did not say you needed such a device. Anyhow, I will arrange the equipment.

(Banging of doors etc. Five minutes later)

O: There we are.

J: I'm ever so sorry. I didn't mean to trouble you. Thank you, young lady. Now, back to our invention. Here is a diagram of the model in front of you. Look at the model itself. Now I will connect the water.

A: I thought you said it was a burglar alarm. Does the burglar get a bath free of charge, or what?

J: My dear lady, what happens when a burglar alarm goes off?

A: There's a loud noise.

J: And what happens when the poor home-owner is deaf?

B: He gets robbed, of course.

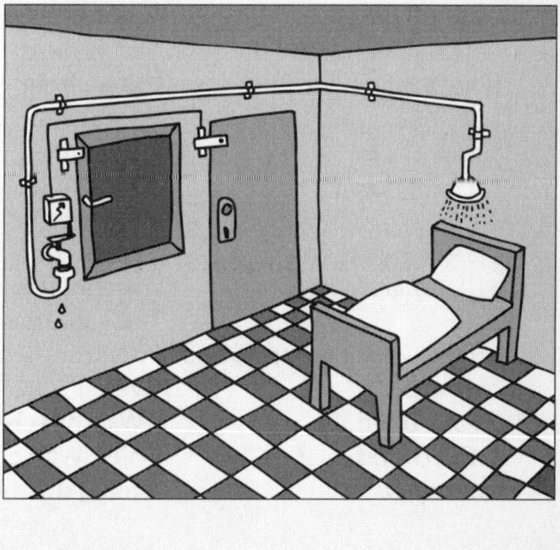

R: Thank you, Bryan, for your cutting sense of humour.
B: My pleasure.
J: That's the point, my friends. Water wakes the deaf sleeper. When someone breaks in, through door or window, a special spray begins to pour on the sleeping, unsuspecting house-owners. Voilà!
(Professor turns tap, water sprays through window of the model and in every direction)
A: Oh, that's pretty!
B: Pretty waterworks.
(Water sprays in Ortrud's face)
O: Oh dear. Look at that. I'm wet through.
J: I'm the most awfully sorry, young lady. You see, these mishaps are only teething problems. And now to the details ...

(V) Vocabulary to help you with the text

advertising sheets	Seiten, Bögen mit Anzeigen
apologise	sich entschuldigen
burglar alarm	Alarmanlage
connect the water	das Wasser anschließen
cutting sense of humour	scharfer Sinn für Humor
deaf	taub
doctorate	Doktortitel
free of charge	umsonst, gratis
in advance	im voraus
metal pipe	Metallrohr
pity about that idea!	Schade um die Idee!
pour	gießen
shift the chairs	die Stühle umstellen
tap	(Wasser-) Hahn
teething problems	Kinderkrankheiten
UK (United Kingdom)	Vereinigtes Königreich von Großbritannien
unsuspecting house-owners	nichtsahnende Hausbesitzer
valve	Ventil
wash-basin	Waschbecken
waterworks	hier: Wasserspiele
wet through	völlig durchnäßt

B Task 1: Word Watch

Once again: Find the functions

1) What speech functions does the chairman use to open the meeting and to announce its purpose? (2)

2) How do the participants apologise? (5)

3) How do they react to the apologies? (5)

(solutions see page 76)

B Task 2: Brain Test

How good is your memory? More than one answer may be correct.

1) Where and when did Professor Jikon invent the burglar alarm?

a That was in the UK, eighty years ago.
b He didn't invent it himself.
c It was in the USA, eighty years ago

2) Professor Jikon used the following media:

a a tap and a model
b a model and an OHP
c a tap, a model and an OHP

3) This is how the burglar alarm functions:

a The model is connected to a tap and water sprays into the model and wakes the sleeper.
b When someone breaks in, a spray begins to pour on the sleepers.
c When there is a noise a tap is turned and water begins to run.

(solutions in the appendix)

Back to Task 1 – Here's the result of our word-watching

Words used by the chairperson

Ladies and gentlemen, may I open this meeting now?

The reason for our coming together is ...

How to apologise

I do beg your pardon.

I do apologise young lady!

I'm terribly/most awfully sorry.

I do regret that I was unable to be here earlier.

I am ever so sorry. It won't happen again.

How to react to apologies

Please don't worry. These things happen.

I quite understand. Don't worry about it.

That's all right. We all make mistakes, don't we?

Never mind!

It doesn't matter.

B Task 3: Form and function

Tick off the most exaggerated form of apology.

- I'm terribly sorry.
- I'm most awfully sorry.
- I am ever so sorry.

Time for a smile: Modern technology

I flew over on the Concorde. That plane is so fast it gives you an extra couple of hours to look for your luggage.

Bob Hope

B Task 4: Match work

Below you see five possible room layouts. Match them against the purpose of the meeting.

	room layout		**function**
1)	Half-circle; no table	**a**	Problem solving and decision taking. Use of visual aids limited.
2)	Classroom style	**b**	Good for larger numbers. Good for demonstrations of real objects.
3)	Conference table	**c**	A brainstorm among the engineers of the R&D Department
4)	Round table	**d**	Listening to the company guru or doing autogenous training.
5)	Horseshoe	**e**	Briefing of larger audiences using OHP or video

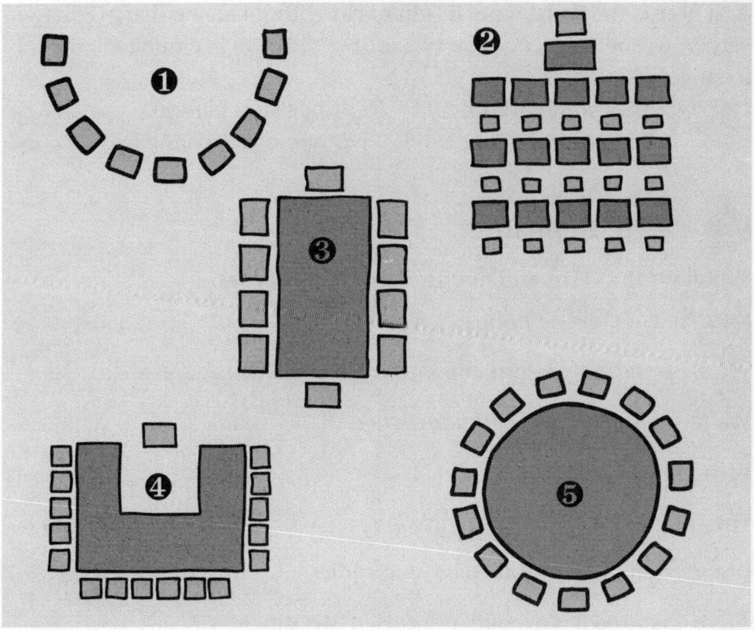

B Task 5: Memory work

1) What did you think was the original room layout in our story?
2) After they had rearranged chairs and tables, what did the room look like?

L Language box: Highlighting and emphasising

You know already two types (see page 40). **First type**: Start with *what* and emphasise the object.

What we need to know are *figures*.

Second type: Start with *It is/was (+ that)* ...

Dr. Hill wanted to know the *costs of promotion*
It was the costs *(that)* Dr. Hill wanted to know.

And here is the **third type**: In sentences without an auxiliary (Hilfsverben wie be, have, do) you can use *do, did, does* to emphasise the following verb.

I *beg* your pardon.	I *do* beg your pardon.
I *apologise*, young lady!	I *do* apologise, young lady!

B Task 6: Emphasise

Highlight the verbs and nouns. Use all three types.

Miss Fünkner, please *bring* in a flip-chart. ....

We *expected* more information. ....

We're suggesting *cuts in production*. ....

I *see* a need for change. ....

They propose a *major reorganisation*. ....

I *regret* that I was unable to be here earlier. ....

More investment is needed, not cuts in investment. ....

B Task 7: Patch work – How to apologise and to forgive

ever		apologise		matter
	do regret		mind	
understand		worry		beg
	all right		awfully sorry	

Put the patches in the right places.

I do .... your pardon.

Never .... ! I'm to blame too.

I do .... , young lady!

Please don't .... These things happen.

I am .... so sorry.

It doesn't .... Things like these tend to happen.

I'm most .... It won't happen again.

That's .... We all make mistakes, don't we?

I .... that I was unable to be here earlier.

I quite .... Don't worry about it.

B Task 8: Match work – What went wrong?

Here are a few sentences overheard during the presentation. Each was provoked by mistakes the presenter made.

speech	function
1) I certainly can't see anything.	**a** Splitting attention instead of focusing it
2) Here is a diagram of the model. And look at the model in front of you.	**b** wrong room layout
3) For my demonstration I need a tap. Have you an OHP?	**c** no preparation

(F) How to handle *disasters*

It was a disaster, wasn't it? It was not the invention, (which, by the way, was a real one) – but the presenter was not prepared at all. The layout of the room, the OHP, the water – everything had to be arranged during the meeting. And then poor Ortrud, was *soaked* to her *bones* by the watery burglar alarm.

Of course, things like that wouldn't happen to you! But what do you do when the flipchart falls over, when there is a *blackout* or the computer program breaks down. Well, what could *damage* your presentation is not the disaster itself – the short interruption of the *flow of your speech* – but your reaction to it: your *confusion*, helplessness or shame.

The best way of handling *minor* catastrophes is a joke or a witty quotation. *In the case of* the first disaster I usually quote Murphy's Law: "If anything can go wrong, it will." And when I *fumble* for a OHP transparency that has mysteriously disappeared I quote the first *amendments* to the above law: "Nothing is as easy as it looks" or "Everything takes longer than you think."

In the rare *event* of a chain of disasters, let's suppose the flipchart falls over and the table collapses so that coffee is spilled over the director's jacket, you'll win the audience over to your side with: "Left to themselves things tend to go *from bad to worse*" or in the case of the director: "*Matter* will be damaged in direct proportion to its *value*."

The real catastrophe is when you can see them *yawning* or hear their impatient *snuffles and shuffles*. There's not a lot you can do. Sometimes it's a good idea to start a question period before you begin the next part.

Unglück
durchweicht/Knochen
Stromausfall
Schaden
Redefluß
Verwirrung
kleinere
im Fall von
hier: suchen
Zusatz
Fall
immer schlimmer/Materie
Wert
gähnen
Räuspern und Füßescharren

Let's put it to the vote

CONTENTS

Time for a smile

The chairman of the board had to make an important speech[1] at a meeting of shareholders[2], and as usual he delegated the job of writing the speech to his secretary: "Miss Smith, just put something together for me, will you? You know all the facts and figures. And make it short and sweet – about twenty minutes should do."
When he returned to the office after the meeting, he was in a furious[3] temper. "What's the idea of writing me a one-hour speech?" he thundered. "Half of the audience walked out before I'd finished."
"With respect, sir, I wrote you a twenty-minute speech as you told me," replied the secretary. "However, you asked me to make two extra copies."

1 Rede 2 Aktionäre 3 wütend

Let's put it to the vote

(Phone ringing)

R: Hello, Bossybitch speaking.

N: It's me, Norbert. I was trying to ring you yesterday. Well, what's your comment on that Jikon's performance? I almost fell off my chair. I had to bite my tongue to stop laughing.

R: But it's not a laughing matter, Norbert. I was hoping for more. It's all very expensive. We were discussing that yesterday, weren't we?

N: I know, I know. I can hardly sleep at night worrying.

R: Okay, okay calm down. Tomorrow's the discussion. I'm not looking forward to that. And then on Monday we've the next presentation. See you tomorrow. Bye.

Norbert Kleinstück (N), Ronald Bossybitch (R), Amy Fernando (A), Bryan Hemmung (B), Ortrud Gram (O)

N: Gentlemen, gentlemen, could we have a bit of order here?

B: Well, Norbert, you're looking more nervous than normal. Any reason?

N: Just your imagination, Bryan. Nothing at all! I ...

B: Come on now, Norbert. We can ...

N: Look here, Bryan, I don't like being interrupted like this.

B: Okay, okay.

N: Now coming back to what I was saying. I wanted to ask you all for your opinions concerning the last patent that we saw. The burglar alarm.

R: I'd say that the matter was not perfectly organised.

A: As far as I'm concerned I think it was really a giggle. All that water spraying everywhere when the water came through too fast.

O: My dress was wet through.

B: I suggested you took it off, Ortrud.

O: My dear Bryan, I am the office manager, not a striptease queen.

B: Well no, Ortrud, I can believe that.

N: Going back to what I was saying ... may I ask for reactions to Mr Jikon's presentation?

B: Well, in my eyes the whole thing was a joke. Fancy using water to wake people with hearing disabilities. How many people nowadays are so deaf they can't hear an alarm? There are so many devices on the market to help people hear.

R: And how many people are there like that? Not much of a market, I bet.

O: May I come in at this point with a practical matter?

N: Of course, Ortrud. Fire away!

O: It's simple really. Every time the alarm goes off the house-owner has a lot of extra work. Bed-clothes will have to be dried. And perhaps the occupant of the bed will catch pneumenia.

R: You mean pneumonia, Ortrud.

O: It's all the same when your lungs are in pain. I was wondering whether we should go on with these presentations.

N: We've got the message, thank you. I suggest we put it to the vote. Raise your hands if you're in favour of this invention ... *(Mumbling)* ... I see. That's one vote. Thank you, Amy.

R: Right, so we forget that idea. I suggest we call it a day. Thank you, ladies and gentlemen.

(V) Vocabulary to help you with the text

bite one's tongue	sich auf die Zunge beißen
call it a day	Schluß machen
calm down	beruhige dich; sich beruhigen
Fancy!	Stell dir vor!
hearing disabilities	Horschäden
it was really a giggle	es war wirklich lustig
laughing matter	etwas zum Lachen
lungs	Lungen
occupant; the ~ of the bed	der im Bett Liegende
pain	Schmerz
performance	Leistung, Vorstellung
pneumonia	Lungenentzündung
practical matter	praktische Angelegenheit
revise	wiederholen
we've got the message.	wir haben verstanden

Food for thought: The KISS rule for presenters

Entia non sunt multiplicanda praeter necissatem (Wilhelm von Ockham). This is known as Ockham's razor. It has become the the KISS rule for presenters. In plain English it reads: : Keep It Simple and Stupid

B Task 1: Word watch

Back to our friends. Look at the language of their meeting and find the functions.

1) Nob wants to find out what the team think about Dr Jikon's invention. What words does he use? (3)
2) How do Bryan, Ron and Amy introduce their opinions about the invention? (3)
3) How does Nob react to Bryan's interruption? (2)
4) How does Ortrud interrupt Ronald? (1)
5) How does Nob try to keep up discipline? (1)
6) How does Nob handle the vote?(3)
7) How does he close the meeting? (1)
(solutions see page 86)

B Task 2: Form and function

Tick off the politest or weakest form of interruption.

- Excuse me, could I just break in a moment here ...?
- May I interrupt you for a moment ...?
- Excuse me, sir, may I ask a question?
- I wonder if I might comment upon your last argument?
- Excuse me, but may I just draw your attention to the fact that ...?

Tick off the strongest form of reaction to an interruption.

- If I might just finish my sentence.
- Perhaps I could return to your question later on ...
- I don't like being interrupted like this.
- With respect, I should like to add only this ...

(solutions in the appendix)

B Task 3: Match work – Ending a meeting with a vote

speech	function
1) Well, I think we've covered everything.	a asking for a vote
2) The motion is carried by seven votes to four.	b counting the votes
3) Those in favour say 'Aye'.	c announcing the result
4) Could we move to a vote on this?	d announcing the end of the meeting

B Task 4: Patch work

interrupted		going back		as far as I'm
	in my eyes		I'd say	
may I come		opinions		comment
	put it		reactions	

Can you fit the patches into the right gaps?

Well, what's your .... on that Jikon's performance?

We wanted to ask you all for your .... concerning ...

May I ask for .... to Mr Jikon's presentation?

.... the whole thing was a joke.

.... concerned; I think it was really a giggle.

.... that the matter was not perfectly organised.

.... in at this point with a practical matter?

Look here, Bryan, I don't like being .... like this.

.... to what I was saying... may I ask for reactions to Mr Jikon's presentation?

I suggest we .... to the vote.

Back to Task 1 – Here's the result of our word-watching

How to find out what they think

Well, what's your comment on that Jikon's performance?
We wanted to ask you all for your opinions concerning ...
May I ask for reactions to Mr Jikon's presentation?

How to say what you think

In my eyes the whole thing was a joke.
As far as I'm concerned I think it was really a giggle.
I'd say that the matter was not perfectly organised.

Interrupting and being interrupted

May I come in at this point with a practical matter?
Look here, Bryan, I don't like being interrupted like this.
Going back to what I was saying ... may I ask for reactions to Mr Jikon's presentation?

How to chair the meeting

Could we have a bit of order here?
I suggest we put it to the vote.
Raise your hands if you're in favour of this invention.
I see. That's one vote. Thank you, Amy.
I suggest we call it a day.

Language box: How to be open and friendly

When you use the simple past for facts and events you see them as finished and complete. When you use the progressive form of the verb you appear to be more flexible and open for compromise.

Simple Past	Past Progressive
I tried to ring you yesterday.	I was trying to ring you yesterday.

If you start your sentence with the past progressive of verbs like wonder, hope, discuss, expect etc. your statement is more friendly and open to negotiation. There are two more examples of this kind in the dialogue. Can you find them?

B Task 5: Mind your manners – Be more friendly

Use *wonder if/whether, hope* where necessary and the progressive.

1) I hoped for more.	I .... for more.
2) We should go on with the presentation.	................................we should go on with the presentation.
3) We intended to make new arrangements for next year.	We .... to make new arrangements for next year.
4) Have you come to a decision?	.... if you'd come to a decision yet.
5) We discussed that yesterday, didn't we?	We .... that yesterday, ... ?

B Task 6: Translation exercise – Opinions

Was ist euer Kommentar zu Dr. Jikons Auftritt?

....

Wir wollten nach eurer Meinung über Dr. Jikons Patent fragen.

....

Darf ich um Reaktionen zu Dr. Jikons Präsentation bitten?

....

In meinen Augen war das Ganze ein Witz.

....

Was mich anbelangt, ich denke, es war wirklich lachhaft.

....

Ich würde sagen, die Sache war nicht perfekt organisiert.

....

Darf ich an dieser Stelle etwas Praktisches anmerken?

....

Ich möchte nicht, daß man mich auf diese Art unterbricht.

....

(Lösungen siehe Key to Task 4 im Anhang)

(F) Meetings in Britain

"Have they got the 'meetomania'? Aren't they *exaggerating* it a bit with all these meetings?" you might have been wondering.
Well, Ronald, Amy and Bryan are British and in Britain the meeting is the most important and *time-consuming* management *tool*. It is considered as a part of the work and not as a *necessary evil*. Even unimportant decisions are discussed, voted and *put into practice*.
An important meeting is *scheduled* well in advance and a detailed agenda is *distributed* to all participants. Not everybody will have read it or come to the meeting well-prepared. However, everybody is expected to make a contribution, if only by asking questions, giving his opinion and listening patiently to the *views* of colleagues.
Only the most formal meetings are opened and closed on time. The majority of meetings are informal in style and begin and end with small talk. However, it is not acceptable to leave in the middle of a meeting, make or take phone calls or get on with paperwork.
Discussions may be *controversial*. But it is the chairperson's *concern* to avoid *irreconcilable* clashes. Loyalty to the boss and the company is stronger than even fundamental disagreement.
A meeting without some concrete result is regarded as a *failure*. However, it is considered fair play not to influence members beforehand in order to *bring about* a decision with the help of a lobby. It is usual first to listen to the arguments of the others and then *support* a suggestion.
Of course, there may be some *exceptions* to the rule, especially in politics. After all, it was a Brit who invented the Lobby.

übertreiben
zeitraubend
Instrument
notwendiges Übel
verwirklichen
ansetzen
verteilen
Beitrag
Ansichten
kontrovers
Sorge/unversöhnlich
Mißerfolg
herbeiführen
unterstützen
Ausnahme

More about British business culture in John Mole *Mind Your Manners.* Nicholas Brealy Publishing. London 1995

(F) The chairperson's crossword puzzle

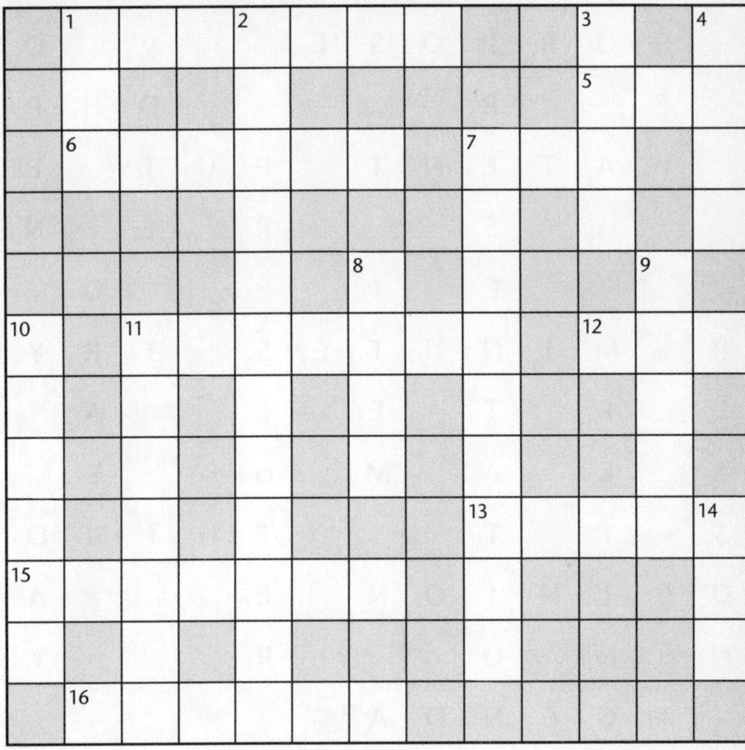

Across

1 This is the ? of our meeting.
5 short for overhead projector
6 certificate for new ideas
7 Let's ...?... it to the vote!
11 written report of the meeting
12 English for *versuchen*
13 first, second, ...?...
15 another word for *view, position*
16 list of items to be discussed
14 Let's call it a ...?... !

Down

1 our first invention
2 process of giving information to an audience
3 Let's have a ...?... on it!
4 I declare the meeting ...?... .
7 man or woman who explains ideas to audiences
8 an issue on the agenda
9 chairpersons must keep it up
10 purpose (of a meeting)
11 chairman opens and closes it

(for the solution, please turn over)

	1 P	U	R	2 P	O	S	E			3 V		4 O
	P			R						5 O	H	P
	6 P	A	T	E	N	T		7 P	U	T		E
				S				R		E		N
				E		8 I		E			9 O	
10 R		11 M	I	N	U	T	E	S		12 T	R	Y
E		E		T		E		E			A	
A		E		A		M		N			E	
S		T		T				13 T	H	I	R	14 D
15 O	P	I	N	I	O	N		E				A
N		N		O				R				Y
	16 A	G	E	N	D	A						

Time for a smile: Modern technology

I hate those answering machines which advise you in a 30-second pre-recorded speech that you will have 10 seconds to talk when you hear the beep in 5 seconds.

Sam Levenson

The wind in the pillows

CONTENTS

Our story: The wind in the pillows
Focus: How to make suggestions
Language box: The grammar of suggestions
Brain work: Let's practise proposing and suggesting
Follow-up: Meetings in Italy

Time for a smile

Mr Jikon's latest invention was a mini burglar-alarm against pick-pockets[1]. Unfortunately it went off in the middle of an opera. Four of spear carriers[2] threw their spears at him.

1 Taschendiebe 2 Speerträger

The wind in the pillows

(The telephone is ringing for Norbert Kleinstück)

N: Hi, it's me. What's new?

R: I've got to go to England on business this week. Can you take care of the meeting?

N: What's it going to be about this week?

R: I suggest that you call it *The Wind in the Pillows*.

N: *The Wind in the Willows*? By Terrence Rattigan? We're not going to promote any novels, are we?

R: In the pillows! It's not the novel, it's a pneumatic wake-up system and burglar alarm.

N: A burglar alarm! Not again! ...

Friday afternoon. At the I.C.S. office. Norbert Kleinstück (N), Bryan Hemmung (B), Amy Fernando (A), Ortrud Gram (O)

B: Nice sign on the wall, Norbert. Plants everywhere. Things are beginning to move in this young company.

A: Yes, it's so fresh in here. I'm really beginning to like it.

O: Yes. And everything is more or less in order. And that's what I like.

B: If I may make a suggestion, we could frame all these funny inventions, hang them up on the wall and have a good laugh from time to time.

N: Well, I'm happy you're all feeling so positive. Ronald will not be with us. He has an appointment in England.

B: Lucky devil! Where's the famous Annette Säuli?

N: She had to accompany Ronald.

B: I bet she did.

N: Never mind. We can manage without them. Today I want to discuss this invention with you all. I've called you together to have an extraordinary meeting to discuss an invention we received yesterday. You have copies of the patent, don't you? Have you read it?

A: I didn't get time. I had some exams to do.

O: I was able to process the text.

B: Oh, you processed it, did you, Ortrud? Well, I hope it didn't give you indigestion.

O: What do you mean?

N: I'm sure Bryan doesn't know what he means.

O: Why don't we put the text of the patent on the OHP?

UNITED STATES PATENT OFFICE
4,031,711
June 28, 1977.
Cold Air Blast Wake-Up Apparatus
Inventor: Peter MacNeil, Mountain St., Montreal, Quebec, Canada.
Filed: May 24, 1976.

Various devices have heretofore been used for waking up an individual from sleep at a predetermined time. Such devices as alarm clocks and clock radios have not proved adequately effective to awaken certain individuals having a low sensitivity to aural stimulus when sleeping. The problem is particularly acute in regard to the deaf.
Wake-up apparatus includes an elongated hose having a funnel member at one end for coupling to the output side of a room air conditioner and a horizontally elongated rectangular outlet on the other end for placement on a mattress for directing air therealong. A rotatable damper vane mounted in the hose is controlled by a motor energised via an electric timer for driving the vane to an open position at a predetermined time for causing a blast of cold air along the mattress.

N: Does anybody have problems with the meaning here in the text?

A: Yes, what's an elongated hose?

B: Just a long hose, Amy.

A: Okay. What's a "motor energised via an electric timer"?

N: That means the motor gets energy regulated by a timer.

B: Stone me! There's Norbert teaching native speaker, Amy, about English words!

N: Back to the invention! Let me show you a foil of the invention. There you are!

N: So you see how it works.

B: What a sadistic device! You set the timer; you're lying in bed in the morning. Then suddenly you get a blast of cold air in your unmentionables.

N: Well, you could get it in your face if you put your feet on the pillow and your head at the foot-end of the bed, so to speak.

A: Oh, that sounds kinky!

B: Norbert, have you gone out of your tiny mind? In my eyes it's time we really started to see reality! Brilliant. Sleep upside down to get a blast of air in the morning. And we have to listen to this late on Friday afternoon!

O: Do you think it might be a good idea to send this patent to that Prof. Nikon with his Bed-Wetting Burglar Alarm.

B: That's it, Ortrud. Then if somebody happened to break in, the sleeper would probably catch double pneumonia ...

A: Well, sometimes I think we're all wasting our time.

B: You can say that again! I suggest going to the Irish pub round the corner and having a pint of Guinness or two.

(V) Vocabulary to help you with the text

acute	akut
adequately effective	angemessen wirksam
air blast	Luftschwall
appointment	Termin, Verabredung
aural stimulus	akustischer Stimulus
couple (v.)	anschließen
deaf	taub
elongated hose	verlängerter Schlauch
energised by	angetrieben durch
frame	Rahmen
funnel	Trichter
heretofore	bis heute (veraltet)
indigestion	Verdauungsstörung
kinky	verrückt, pervers
mounted	montiert
pillow	Kissen
placement	Befestigung
pneumatic	pneumatisch, lufthydraulisch
predetermined time	vorbestimmte Zeit
process the text	den Text bearbeiten; hier: lesen
promote novels	für Romane werben
rectangular outlet	rechteckige Öffnung
rotatable damper vane	drehbarer dämpfender Ventilator
sensitivity	Empfindlichkeit
Stone me!	Ich werd' verrückt!
The Wind in the Willows	Der Wind in den Weiden (Roman von T. Rattigan)
tentative	versuchsweise, behutsam
unmentionables	die Unaussprechlichen (Unterhosen)
various devices	verschiedene Geräte, Vorrichtungen
waste time	Zeit verschwenden

B Task 1: Word watch

Back to our friends. Look at the language of their meeting and find the ten functions.

1) What words does Nob use to create a friendly atmosphere? (1)
2) How does he excuse absent members? (1)
3) How does he announce the reason for the meeting? (2)
4) In the dialogue the participants make suggestions. How do they introduce them? (6)

(solutions see page 98)

B Task 2: Brain test

Again more than one answer might be correct.

1) The team feels positive today because
a there are potted plants everywhere.
b there are framed patents hanging on the wall.
c the office has been tidied up.

2) Why is Ronald Bossybitch not at the meeting?
a He is listening to the wind in the willows with T. Rattigan.
b He has an appointment with T. Rattigan.
c He is on a business trip to England

3) Let's have a look at the patent. The sleeper is awakened by a stream of air. Where does it come from?
a from a fan
b from the air conditioning
c from a rectangular outlet in the window

4) Why does the inventor use a blast of wind to alarm the sleeper?
a Some people are so fast asleep that they don't hear an acoustic alarm.
b A normal burglar alarm would be heard by the burglar, too.
c It is a burglar alarm for deaf people.

(solutions in the appendix)

B Task 3: Form and function

Tick off the most tentative (vorsichtige) form of suggestion.

- ▪ I would suggest that you call it The Wind in the Pillows.
- ▪ If I may make a suggestion, we could send it to Dr. Nikon.
- ▪ Why don't we put the text of the patent on the OHP?
- ▪ I suggest going to the Irish pub round the corner.

B Task 4: Complete the joke

The wife of a rich American banker received[1] the following phone call from a gang who had kidnapped her husband.
"We demand one million dollars as a ransom[2] for your husband.
We ....[3] pay or you'll never see him again."
After a moment's thought the woman replied[4]: "Well, may I ....
.... a compromise? You will get the money on the condition[5] that you keep my husband."

B Task 5: Match work

In the two columns you find tentative, neutral and strong forms of making a suggestion: Do you think you can match them off?

1)	I strongly recommend that ...	**a**	What about ... ?
2)	Why don't we ... ?	**b**	I recommend that ...
3)	I wonder if I might suggest ...	**c**	I advise you most strongly to ...
4)	I propose that ...	**d**	If I might make a suggestion.

Time for a smile: Modern technology

I put the wrong size of batteries in the beeper[6] that I wear on my belt. The first call I got blew my shoes off[7].

1 erhalten 2 Lösegeld 3 empfehlen Ihnen 4 antworten 5 Bedingung 6 Piepser 7 weg-, absprengen

Back to Task 1 – Here's the result of our word-watching

Words the chairman has used

Well, I'm happy you're all feeling so positive.
Ronald will not be with us. He has an appointment in England.
I've called you together to have an extraordinary meeting to discuss an invention we received yesterday.
Today I want to discuss this invention with you all.

How to make a suggestion

I suggest that you call it The Wind in the Pillows.
I suggest going to the Irish pub round the corner.
I suggest that the girls hang up those inventions.
Why don't we put the text of the patent on the OHP?
If I may make a suggestion, we could frame those patents.
Do you think it might be a good idea to send it to Dr. Nikon?

(L) Language box: The grammar of suggestions

1) I suggest + ing-form
I suggest *going* to the Irish pub round the corner.
Der Sprecher schließt sich in den Vorschlag mit ein.

2) I suggest that you (should) + infinitive
I suggest that *you call it* "The Wind in the Pillows".
Der Sprecher macht anderen einen Vorschlag.

3) Infinitive without to
Why *don't we take* an early flight ...?
Why not take an early flight?

4) Question word + ing-form
What about going to the Irish pub?
How about framing the inventions and hanging them on the walls?

Let's practise that immediately. To complicate things we have included other structures as well.

B Task 6: Patch work

we send		to ask		read
	putting		take	
should reject		applying		to wait
	asking		we apply	

Can you fit the patches into the right gaps?

I suggest that .... for the patent immediately.

I suggest .... for more information first.

Why not .... a look at other inventions?

Why don't .... this invention back to Professor Jikon?

Wouldn't it be a good idea if you .... the handout first?

Wouldn't it be a good idea .... for an interview?

How about .... for a bank loan?

I recommend that we .... this Invention.

I recommend .... more flowers in the office.

Wouldn't it be better .... until Ronald gets back?

Food for thought

There is no great genius without some touch of madness.

Seneca

(F) Meetings in Italy

The participants

According to John Mole[1] meetings in Italy may start with three or four people, a few more may come in, a few more may go. It might not always be clear why some people are there at all. Sometimes you get the *impression* that meetings are merely social gatherings to *reinforce* a sense of *togetherness*.

nach Meinung
Eindruck verstärken
Gemeinschaft

The agenda

It is difficult to *impose* an agenda, although it is always *worthwhile* trying if you are in a position to do so. Otherwise discussion may be *interminable*. A large *proportion* of meetings end without a satisfactory *conclusion*, in which case they are *reconvened*.

aufzwingen
der Mühe wert
endlos
Anteil
Abschluß/wieder aufnehmen

The discussion

A meeting is often a stage for *exhibiting eloquence*, personality and status and is consequently a free-for all opinions, comment and ideas. Everyone is *entitled* to make a contribution, is listened to and apparently agreed with. The *weight* of the idea *resides* not in the idea itself but in the importance and *influence* of the speaker.

Redegewandtheit/zur Schau stellen/berechtigt
Gewicht/liegen
Einfluß

Lobbying

If a proposal is to be put to a meeting it is often *advisable* to *clear* it with each of the participants beforehand. Then they will react constructively. If a new idea is *sprung* on a meeting everyone will automatically *object*. A process of open decision-making is illusory.

ratsam/abklären
überraschen
dagegen sein

1 Adapted from John Mole *Mind Your Manners*. Nicholas Brealy Publishing. London 1995

The Japanese make them smaller and cheaper

CONTENTS

Our story: The Japanese make them smaller and cheaper
Focus: How to avoid misunderstandings
Brain work: Asking for information – giving information
Language box: Make sure you got the message: question tags
Follow-up: Meetings in Japan

Time for a smile: The truth about meetings

If you explain so clearly that nobody can misunderstand, somebody will.

It is not necessary to understand things in order to argue about[1] them.

1 um zu streiten über

The Japanese make them smaller and cheaper

N: *(fade in)* ... so the whole meeting didn't go very well. The others were all angry in the end. They wanted to know if our little enterprise was just a complete joke.

R: And how did you calm the situation down?

N: Well, I'm afraid I got completely nervous and upset.

R: How unusual! Never mind! What's the position now?

N: Ortrud stepped in. We have a meeting tomorrow and she's bringing somebody along.

Tuesday 10 a.m. The I.C.S. office. Ronald Bossybitch (R), Norbert Kleinstück (N), Amy Fernando (A), Bryan Hemmung (B), Ortrud Gram (O), Mr Yudeedit (Y)

O: Thank you for coming, gentlemen. In the last weeks we have had a lot of inventions, patents and many disappointments. In our last meeting some of you were getting desperate.

B: Oh, you noticed, did you, Ortrud?

O: Today it is my great pleasure to introduce Mr Yudeedit, from Tokyo, Japan. Mr Yudeedit, welcome to ICS in Heidelberg.

Y: Thank you for this friendly welcome. The pleasure is mine, Miss Gram. How do you do, ladies and gentlemen?

All: How do you do?

O: Let me explain the background to you. You were all a bit depressed at the last meeting. I described the situation to my husband. He works in the subsidiary of a Japanese software company. Mr Yudeedit is from a software house in Japan and he was visiting my husband's company here. Mr Yudeedit, the floor is yours.

Y: Thank you, Mrs Gram. In Japan we have developed a completely new service.

R: Could you be a little more precise, Mr Doyutit? What is your invention exactly?

Y: Yudeedit actually.

R: Beg your pardon. Who did what?

Y: Yudeedit – my name pronounced correctly. Well, what is the product? That's a very complex question. Let me try to explain. Our service or should I say solution, is Japanese through and through.

B: *(whispering to Amy)* That reminds me of a joke. It's one of Norbert's. "The Italians are the best lovers but the Japanese make them smaller and cheaper."

R: I'm afraid it's not quite clear what you mean by that. Could you tell us some details, Mr Yudeedit?

Y: I'm afraid I haven't enough information at my disposal at the moment. I'll give you a general idea. Then if you're interested I could present IMM to you.

A: Present who?

Y: IMM.

A: Excuse me, but we weren't quite able to catch what you were saying. Who is 'him'?

Y: Perhaps I should make this clearer by saying that IMM is the Intelligent Meet Master. He's two metres tall, weighs 200 kgms, has the best of a new generation of brains, has the gift of speech with a metallic voice and ...

A: Poor fellow. Did he have an operation?

Y: Young lady, IMM is the end product of years of various operations. He moves around slowly, clanks a bit but he's mobile.

A: Poor thing. Does he have arthritis or something? And what did Bryan mean by "he is smaller and cheaper than an Italian"?

B: *(laughing)* It occurs to me that there is some misunderstanding going on here. IMM is some sort of machine, isn't he?

Y: With respect, that is not what I said! Not some sort of machine. He is the intelligent computerised robot! The robotised computer!

N: My goodness. My goodness me! What does he do?

O: Mr Yudeedit, perhaps you could continue.

Y: IMM takes care of meetings and conferences. His talents include controlling meetings, translating and interpreting. He speaks 72 different languages. He takes the minutes of meetings, has integrated fax and video facilities. He can talk. IMM knows how to manage meetings optimally. And much, much more.

B: Well, stone me! I never expected to hear anything like that in this office.

O: But can this metal man really do all these things?

Y: IMM is the product of years of the best Japanese research. How could he not succeed? By the way, a female model will be available soon.

R: Mr Yudonit ...

Y: Yudeedit, actually.

R: I beg your pardon. Could you make a presentation for us? As soon as possible.

Y: It will be my pleasure. It will be our pleasure, IMM's and mine.

(V) Vocabulary to help you with the text and the exercises

available	vorhanden, verfügbar
calm the situation down	die Wogen glätten
catch a word	ein Wort verstehen
confirmation	Bestätigung
cross purposes; be at ~	aneinander vorbeireden
depressed	deprimiert
desperate	verzweifelt
disappointment	Enttäuschung
disposal; have something at one's ~	etwas zur Verfügung haben
enterprise	Unternehmen
facilities	Möglichkeiten, Einrichtungen
gift of speech	die Gabe der Sprache
include	einschließen, umfassen
minutes of the meeting	Protokoll der Besprechung
my goodness!	du meine Güte!
occur; it occurs to me	mir kommt der Gedanke; mir fällt auf / ein
research	Forschung
step in	einspringen, aushelfen
subsidiary	Tochtergesellschaft
succeed	erfolgreich sein, Erfolg haben
translate	übersetzen
upset	verwirrt, verstört, schockiert
various	verschiedene
voice	Stimme

B Task 1: Word watch

Back to our friends. Look at the language of their meeting and find out the 17 functions.

1) How does Ortrud introduce Mr Yudeedit? (2)
2) How does she invite him to address the team? (2)
3) How do the members of the meeting ask for more information? (4)
4) How does Mr Yudeedit announce that he is going to give new information? (3)
5) How do the members of the meeting react to misunderstandings? (6)
(solution see page 106)

B Task 2: Brain test

Again more than one answer might be correct.

1) Mr Yudeedit works
- **a** in a subsidiary of a Japanese software company.
- **b** in the Japanese company where Ortrud's husband works.
- **c** for a Japanese software house.
- **d** for IMM Ltd.

2) IMM has the following functions:
- **a** He chairs meetings.
- **b** He controls meetings.
- **c** He keeps the minutes.

3) How many languages does IMM speak?
- **a** 72
- **b** 27
- **c** 14

(solutions in the appendix)

Time for a smile: The truth about meetings

A committee is twelve men doing the work of one.

Back to Task 1 – Here's the result of our word-watching

How to handle guest speakers

It is my great pleasure to introduce Mr Yudeedit, from Tokyo.
Mr Yudeedit, welcome to ICS in Heidelberg.
Mr Yudeedit, the floor is yours.
Mr Yudeedit, perhaps you could continue.

How to ask for information

What is your invention exactly?
Could you be a little more precise?
Could you tell us some details, Mr Yudeedit?
I'm afraid it's not quite clear what you mean by that.

Giving information

Let me explain the background to you.
Let me try to explain.
I'll give you a general idea. Then if you're interested I could present IMM to you.

How to avoid or react to misunderstandings

It occurs to me that there is some misunderstanding going on here.
I'm afraid we weren't quite able to catch what you were saying.
With respect, that is not what I said.
I'm afraid there seems to have been a slight misunderstanding.
I'm afraid I didn't express myself clearly.
Perhaps I should make this clearer by saying that IMM is the Intelligent Meet Master.

B Task 3: Form and function

Which participant asks the presenter to explain again what he has just said?

A: It depends on what you mean by IMM.
N: If I've understood you correctly, you're saying that IMM can talk.
R: Am I correct in assuming that IMM is some sort of machine?

B Task 4: Match work – How to get the message

speech	function
1) If I've understood you correctly, you're saying that ... ?	a asking for repetition
2) I'm afraid we weren't quite able to catch what you were saying.	b asking for confirmation
3) We seem to be talking at cross purposes.	c clearing up misunderstandings
4) Let me put it this way ... In simpler terms ...	d signalling misunderstanding

F Have you got the message? Increase your word power

How can you make sure that you have understood a speaker correctly?

1) Reformulate what you think the speaker wanted to say.
2) Ask the speaker to confirm your statement.

Here are a few examples:

What you are saying is that it is some sort of machine, aren't you?

Are you saying that this robot can chair meetings?

When you say it's a robotised computer do you mean it controls meetings like a computer?

Would I be right in saying that it IMM is a computerised robot?

Am I correct in assuming that it can take the minutes as well?

If I've understood you correctly, you're saying that it speaks 72 languages?

B Task 5: Mind your manners

Tick off the most polite form of explaining something the second or third time.

- Well then, let me put it this way ...
- I'm probably not making myself clear. Let me put it another way ...
- What I'm trying to say is this: ...

L Language box: The question tag

If you want a person to confirm your statement, you can add a question tag, a form of *be, do, have, can* and other auxiliaries (Hilfsverben). **Regel:** Hilfsverben wie *have, can* (3,4) und *be* und *do* (1,2,6) werden wiederholt; Vollverben werden durch *do* ersetzt (5).

positive statement	negative question tag
1) It'*s* a robot,	*is*n't it?
2) You'*re* from Tokyo,	*are*n't you?
3) You'*ve* bought the robot,	*have*n't you?
4) IMM *can* speak 72 languages,	*can*'t he?
5) You *knew* that he works for us,	*did*n't you?
6) There *is* something ticking inside,	*is*n't there?

negative statement	positive question tag
1) It'*s not* a robot,	*is* it?
2) You *aren't* from Tokyo,	*are* you?
3) You *haven't* bought the robot,	*have* you?
4) IMM *can't* speak 47 languages,	*can* he?
5) You *didn't* know he works for us,	*did* you?
6) There *isn't* anything ticking inside,	*is* there?

B Task 6: Patch work – Getting the message

put		are you		with respect
	purposes		catch	
correctly		slight		doesn't he
	mean		precise	

Can you fit the patches into the right gaps?

Let me .... it this way.

Could you be a little more .... ?

...., that is not what I said.

We seem to be talking at cross ....

Your IMM speaks 72 languages, ... ?

You are not going to buy that robot, ... ?

I'm afraid I'm not quite clear what you .... by that.

I'm afraid there seems to have been a .... misunderstanding.

I'm afraid we weren't quite able to .... what you were saying.

If I've understood you ...., you're saying that IMM is a robot.

Food for thought: The truth about meetings

If you need to have a meeting you are probably fudging an issue[1]. A one-hour meeting for eight people takes a full man-day. Being ill-prepared not only wastes time, it is the height of ill manners[2].

Peter Gummer, Chairman of Shandwick plc,
the world's largest public relation's consultancy

1 einem Problem ausweichen 2 schlechte Manieren

(F) Meetings in Japan

The first meeting

"I'm afraid," said Mr Yudeedit "I haven't enough information *at my disposal* at the moment. I'll give you a general idea. Then if you're interested I could present IMM to you." Mr Yudeedit was of course well prepared. However, in Japan, the first meeting is usually for *preliminary* observation, sort of a Japanese shadow boxing.

zur Verfügung
vorläufig(e)

Time management

Japanese are very *punctual*. Otherwise time is fluid. A meeting will *carry on* until it is finished or interrupted at the *request* of a senior person outside. You should not try to *rush things* or take control. Fast answers are not respected, and long *silences* are normal – they are thinking time.

pünktlich
andauern
Wunsch
drängen
Schweigen

They observe and listen.

If you are making a presentation to Japanese managers, don't watch out for signs of *approval* or *disapproval*. Don't expect them to show their interest by interrupting you with questions. They won't laugh, frown or *cough*. Laughter is seen as a sign of *embarrassment*. They will observe and listen in silence. It is a sign of their respect for your ideas. And if they listen with their eyes closed, it is because they are concentrating on what you are saying.

Beifall
Ablehnung
husten
Verlegenheit

Negotiations in Japan

Don't bring your *lawyers*! They would think that you do not trust them. A contract is an agreement between gentlemen. Personal *relations* are more important than contracts. Lawyers are considered an unnecessary *evil*. Experts, however, are highly respected.

Juristen
Beziehungen
Übel

IMM, the International Meet Master

CONTENTS

Time for a smile: Murphy's Law about meetings

If you are early, it will be cancelled[1].
If you are on time, you will have to wait.
If you are late, you will be too late.
If you leave the room, you are elected[2].

1 absagen 2 wählen

IMM, the International Meet Master

(Telephone rings)

N: It's me, Norbert. What did you think of that Japanese, Yudinut?

R: It's Yudeetit.

N: Complicated names! Why can't they have normal names?

R: Like German ones, I suppose?

N: Hmmph! Anyway, what about his robot?

R: It could be what we're looking for. We'll see tomorrow.

At the ICS office. Ronald Bossybitch (R), Norbert Kleinstück (N), Amy Fernando (A), Bryan Hemmung (B), Ortrud Gramm (O), Mr Yudeedit (Y), IMM (I)

R: Ladies and gentlemen and especially Mr Yudeedit, welcome to our office today. Mr Yudeedit will now speak to you. We're all looking forward to his presentation of what I think is quite an extraordinary little gadget. Mr Yudeedit, over to you.

Y: Thank you very much, but first of all I'd like you to have a look at the handouts in front of you while I'm going through my checklist with Frau Gram. It'll only take a moment.

(He turns to Ortrud)

Do we have an OHP, an electric power point, a round conference table? Has everyone a chair, plus one extra for IMM? OHP sheets numbered. Flip chart. Good, I think that's everything. ...

Okay, ladies and gentlemen, I appreciate that you are willing to sacrifice one hour of your valuable time to listen to me. May I present IMM? Don't hesitate to interrupt IMM when you have a question.

(Knocking at the door. Door opens. IMM strides confidently across the floor. Clanging noises)

I: *(in metallic voice)* How do you all do? I'll be speaking to you in standard English mode, American accent, for exactly 45 minutes and 10 seconds.

B: He looks like something from Star Wars.

Y: There's no reason to be alarmed. IMM looks more aggressive than he actually is.

I: I'm afraid, your statements are only interpretations, gentlemen. Not objective and therefore of little value here. However, I understand your apprehensions but they are unfounded. Let me explain. I would like to present myself. First of all I will give you an overview of my main parts. Then I will describe my major functions. May I draw your attention to the OHP sheet? There you see a simple diagram of myself. Starting at the top of the diagram you see my head. It swivels by 5°. Each turn switches me to another language. I speak 72 languages. I have the most sophisticated software available.

B: I could do with some of that.

I: A worthless suggestion, if I may say so. Your small human brain does not have the capacity.

A: Ha, ha, Bryan has a small brain. I always suspected that.

I: I shall have to call you to order, young lady. Interrupting wastes time. To return to my presentation ... my movable parts are transported by high precision pneumatics. Although my outer casing is of metal, it is a material specially developed for me. I am two metres tall and ...

(Loud bang on the table. Amy and Nob jump; they had been dozing)

A: My God! Has a bomb exploded?

A: It frightened the life out of me.

I: That was merely my function for attracting the attention of participants who are not paying attention. Let me assure you, you need have no fears as long as you concentrate on the matter. Let me now come to my other functions. These include automatic videotaping of the meeting, taking the minutes, translating documentation and interpreting and controlling the meeting to make sure time is not wasted. I also have a language correcting facility. If anybody makes a mistake I can put them right.

B: Translating function. I'm sure Annette will like that. It'll put her out of work.

I: I'm sorry to have to say this, young man, but your comments add nothing to the business of today. We will ignore them.

B: Well, thank you and good bye.

I: Are there any questions, ladies and gentlemen? *(long silence)* Well, if nobody has any further questions *(IMM's voice is getting weaker* *and weaker)* ... if nobody has any further questions ... has any further questions ... further questions ... further ques ... further qu ... qu ... qu ... gg.

Y: Well ladies and gentlemen, you see IMM is a bit tired because we've overdrawn our meeting by ten minutes. I suggest we now draw the presentation to a close. However, if you have any questions or if somebody is interested in having a look at IMM's inner organs, I'll be at your disposal for another hour.

R: Mr Yudeedit, on behalf of our team I would like to thank you and IMM for this most fascinating demonstration of Japanese research and inventiveness. I think everybody will agree that IMM managed it.

(V) Vocabulary to help you with the text

apprehensions	Befürchtungen, Sorgen
appreciate	zu schätzen wissen
attract the attention to	die Aufmerksamkeit lenken auf
automatic videotaping	automatische Videoaufnahme
available	verfügbar, vorhanden
brain	Gehirn
call to order	zur Ordnung rufen
capacity	Kapazität, Speicherplatz
casing	Gehäuse
concentrate on the matter	sich auf die Sache konzentrieren
confidently	selbstsicher, zuversichtlich
correcting facility	Korrektureinrichtung, -funktion
doze	dösen
draw someone's attention to	jemandes Aufmerksamkeit lenken auf
especially	besonders, vor allem
extraordinary	außergewöhnlich

frighten the life out of someone	jemanden zu Tode erschrecken
gadget	Apparat, Vorrichtung
hesitate	zögern
let me assure you	seien Sie versichert
look forward to	sich freuen auf
look for	suchen nach
main parts	wichtige Teile
major functions	wichtige Funktionen
mention	erwähnen
movable parts	bewegliche Teile
noise	Geräusch, Lärm
participant	Teilnehmer
pay attention	aufpassen
please refer to the OHP sheet	betrachten Sie bitte die Folie
pneumatics	Lufthydraulik
put someone out of work	jemanden arbeitslos machen
put someone right	jemanden korrigieren
reason (n.; v.)	Grund; argumentieren
sacrifice	opfern; Opfer
sophisticated	hochentwickelt
statement	Aussage, Erklärung
suspect	vermuten, argwöhnen
switch	(um-)schalten
swivel	sich drehen, schwenken
take the minutes	das Protokoll führen
unfounded	unbegründet
value	Wert
worthless suggestion	wertloser Vorschlag

Time for a smile: Murphy about meetings

If a problem causes many meetings,
the meetings eventually become more
important than the problem.

B Task 1: Word watch

Back to our friends. Look at the language of their meeting and find the 18 functions.

Words used by the chairman

How does Ronald greet the participants of the meeting? (1)
How does he introduce the purpose of the meeting? (1)
How does Mr Yudeedit start his presentation? (2)
How does Yudeedit thank his audience for participating at the presentation? (1)
How does Mr Yudeedit invite the participants to interrupt and ask questions? (1)
How does IMM continue after having been interrupted? (1)
How does IMM discipline his audience? (3)
How is the end of the presentation announced? (1)

B. The language of presentations

How does Mr Yudeedit encourage the audience to interrupt IMM and ask questions? (1)
How does IMM announce his overview and the two parts of his presentation? (3)
How does IMM structure his presentation (draw attention to the OHP sheet its parts and his functions)? (3)
(solutions see page 118)

B Task 2: Brain test

What do you remember of the presentation? Mark these statements either true (T) or false (F).

1) IMM videotapes meetings. [/]
2) He /she prepares the agenda. [/]
3) IMM also takes the minutes of a meeting. [/]
4) IMM corrects wrong grammar and vocabulary. [/]
5) IMM keeps up the discipline of a meeting. [/]

B Task 3: Match work

speech		function	
1)	Mr Brain, will now speak to you.	a	keeping discipline
2)	Mr Brain, over to you.	b	summarising a presentation
3)	I shall have to call you to order.	c	announcing a guest speaker
4)	If I may just go over the main points.	d	making someone take the floor

B Task 4: Patch work

call		value		appreciate
	add		floor	
forward		Starting		First of all
	hesitate		draw	

Can you fit the patches into the right gaps?

.... I will give you an overview of my main parts.

.... at the top of the diagram you see my head.

May I .... your attention to the OHP sheet?

I'm afraid your statement was of little .... here.

Your comments .... nothing to the business of today.

I shall have to .... you to order, young lady.

I .... that you are sacrificing one hour of your valuable time.

Don't .... to interrupt IMM when you have a question.

Mr Yudeedit, the .... is yours.

We're all looking .... to your presentation.

Back to Task 1 –

Here's the result of our word-watching

Words used by the chairman

Ladies and gentlemen, welcome to our office today.
We're all looking forward to a presentation of what I think is quite an extraordinary little gadget.
Mr Yudeedit will now speak to you.
Mr Yudeedit, over to you.
I will now draw the presentation to a close.

How to start the presentation

I appreciate that you are willing to sacrifice one hour of your valuable time.
Don't hesitate to interrupt IMM when you have a question.
May I present IMM?

How to signpost (structure) a presentation

First of all I will give you an overview of my main parts.
Then I will describe my major functions.
Let me now come to my other functions.

How to capture the audience's attention

Starting at the top of the diagram you see my head.
May I draw your attention to the OHP sheet?
To return to my presentation ...

How to keep discipline

I'm afraid your statement was only interpretation. Not objective and therefore of little value here.
I'm sorry to have to say this, young man, but your comments add nothing to the business of today. We'll ignore them.
I shall have to call you to order, young lady.

B Task 5: Guided translation

Let's repeat chapter 3: Speech functions for presenters

In my presentation today I'm going to explain our *(neues Projekt)*

I'll begin my presentation by giving you an *(Überblick)* of the project.

I'm trying to give you a *(Zusammenfassung)* of IMM's functions.

The *(Gegenstand)* of my presentation is our International Meet Master.

In my presentation I'm going to *(erklären)* how to handle the robot.

My presentation will be in three *(Hauptteilen)*.

F A just-in-time checklist for your presentation

Are the visual aids arranged in sequence? ■

Does the overhead projector work properly? ■

Is the overhead projector in focus? ■

Is their enough flip chart paper available? ■

Are there marker pens for the white board? ■

Do you have enough space to move around in? ■

Have you got the right number of handouts? ■

Is the lighting suitable? ■

Time for a smile

A meeting is an event where the minutes are kept[1] and the hours are lost.

Arthur Bloch, Murphy's Laws

1 das Protokoll führen

(F) Meetings in France

There are two types of meetings, those *called* by the manager or the boss and those where there is no *senior figure* present.

einberufen
hochgestellte Person

Meetings called by the manager

The purpose of the meeting is for briefing and coordination. *Unlike* in Great Britain it is neither a forum for debates nor a tool for decision making. You cannot expect problems to be *sorted out* or *trial balloons* to be floated around.
The meeting will follow an *established* format with a detailed agenda. The participants will come well prepared for the *contribution* they are expected to make and they will not be seriously *contradicted*. To *question* an idea or a proposal is to question the competence of the person who *put it forward*.

anders als
lösen/Versuchsballone
feststehend
Beitrag
widersprechen
in Frage stellen
vorbringen

Meetings on the lower level

Spontaneity and creativity take place on the lower level of communication between people who think they can *trust* each other. These meetings are less structured or not structured at all. Participants will feel free to leave the meeting, interrupt each other and speak *simultaneously*. Contributions are *assertive* to the point of being *combative* and phrased to beat back opposition. If a decision is to be taken and some of the *relevant* persons are absent, it will be taken anyway and the others will be informed.

trauen
gleichzeitig/anmaßend/
kämpferisch
wichtig

Adapted from John Mole *Mind Your Manners*. Nicholas Brealy Publishing. London 1995.

Bryan and IMM in Action

CONTENTS

Time for a smile: Murphy's Law about meetings

The length of a meeting rises with the square[1] of the number of people present. Who shouts[2] loudest has the floor[3].

1 im Quadrat 2 schreien 3 das Wort haben

Bryan and IMM in Action

(Telephone rings)

N: What did you think of the Intelligent Meet Master?

R: I'm still getting over the shock. But I reckon it's got a lot of potential.

N: Do you think it's safe? It seemed a bit dominant to me.

R: No problem with that. IMM is certainly the best chance we've had so far. Let's go for it!

(Two days later; the phone rings in the office at ICS)

N: Ronald, I've arranged a meeting with a potential customer, Kufer and Faiter, K&F. They sell software on the international market. Bryan's going to present IMM to them.

R: Okay, but I want to go along to see how he does it and to give support.

At K&F's conference room. Present are: Ronald Bossybitch (R), Bryan Hemmung (B), IMM (I), Mr Kufer (K), Mr Faiter (F) and some managers.

K: Gentlemen, I'd like to thank you all for your time today. As you all know from your pre-conference handouts we'll be having a very unusual meeting today: the presentation of a most exciting piece of hardware. With this in mind I'd like to welcome Mr Bryan Hemmung and Mr Ronald Bossybitch to K&F's premises. And, of course, IMM himself. Mr Hemmung, the floor is yours.

B: Thank you very much, gentlemen for sacrificing some of your valuable time to IMM and me. I'm sure you won't regret it. I've come to talk to you – you've come to listen to me. If you finish first, please let me know.

(Polite laughter)

Well, to start with, can everybody see? If you can move your chairs in a little.

(Chairs moving)

Thank you. As you all know from experience, presenters tend either to talk over the heads of their audience or under their feet. With a little help from IMM I'll try to avoid these pitfalls and ...

I: *(in a metallic voice)* Mr Hemmung, let's not get sidetracked. The issue under discussion is the Intelligent Meet Master. Your output of information equals zero ... And for God's sake stop fidgeting with that biro!

B: Stone me! Well, gentlemen, you see, it works. What was I going to say ... Ah ... Here we are. ... First, I'd like to show you several OHP sheets with details of IMM's working parts and functions. Then, in the second part of the meeting, there will be a period for free discussion and question time. And during this period IMM will participate. I'll use the flipchart here for any spontaneous response or questions which might arise.

F: Well, we'll certainly all look forward to that, Mr Hemmung.

B: So I'll begin if there are no further questions. If you look at the first OHP foil you'll see a diagram of IMM, the Intelligent Meet Master. He ...

K: I'm sorry, Mr Hemmung, could you move to the side, please. It's no problem really but your body's in the way. I can't see the foil.

B: Oh, I'm sorry, of course. I know I'm a bit big ... temporarily at least, but I'm already on a diet, you know. Ha, ha!

I: *(in a metallic voice)* Mr Hemmung, this is your third attempt at being funny. Could you keep to the point, please? I will print some rules on making a presentation from one of my files. Please wait five seconds.

B: Well, thank you for your support, IMM, but I guess I won't wait. Gentlemen, please allow me to continue ...

(Fade out; murmuring going on in the background; fade in)

... And so now I'll bring the first part of our presentation to an end.

F: Well, we'd like to thank you for the information, Mr Hemmung. I'm sure we all found it very interesting indeed. Perhaps we could now begin with question time if you're ready, gentlemen, or shall we have a short break of ...?

I: If I may interrupt, I suggest beginning immediately. This saves valuable time. Mr Faiter, I believe you are most senior here. Please make your comment.

R: Don't worry, gentlemen, IMM seems to be a little impatient, but ...

I: Mr Bossybitch, it is not a question of impatience. It is a matter of time and efficiency. Mr Faiter, please continue ...

(V) Vocabulary to help you with the text

amplify	vergrößern, verstärken
arise; questions ~	Fragen tauchen auf
avoid a pitfall	eine Falle umgehen
by heart	auswendig
call a spade a spade	die Dinge beim Namen nennen
consider	betrachten, in Betracht ziehen
doze off	einnicken
efficiency	Effizienz, Leistungsfähigkeit
fidget	nervös herumfummeln
file	Datei; Ordner
get sidetracked	hier: vom Thema abkommen
give support	unterstützen
grateful	dankbar
have a lot of potential	hier: vielversprechend sein
implications	Folgen, Konsequenzen
introductory words	einführende Worte
opportunity	Gelegenheit
option	Wahl, Alternative
pointer	Zeiger
potential customer	möglicher Kunde
pre-conference handouts	Tischvorlagen, die vor einer Besprechung verteilt werden
premises	Firmenräume, -gelände
print	ausdrucken
propose	vorschlagen
reckon	annehmen
response	Reaktion
sacrifice (v.; n.)	opfern; Opfer
suck	saugen
talk over someone's head	über jemandes Kopf hinweg reden
tap on the foil	auf die Folie klopfen
vacuum cleaner	Staubsauger

B Task 1: Word watch

Back to IMM and Bryan Hemmung. Look at the language of their meeting and find the thirteen functions.

A. The words a chairperson might use

1) How do Mr Faiter and Bryan thank the participants for attending the meeting? (2)
2) How does Mr Faiter announce the purpose of the meeting? (1)
3) How does Mr Faiter greet the representatives of ICS? (1)
4) How does he ask Bryan to start his presentation? (1)
5) How does IMM call Bryan to order? (2)

B. The words a presenter might use

1) How does Bryan check whether the layout of the room is alright? (1)
2) How does he prepare the audience for the visuals he is going to use? (2)
3) How does he structure the presentation? (3)
(solutions see page 126)

B Task 2: Match work – Word power

Match the speech functions that have almost the same meaning.

1) I'm grateful to have the chance to speak to you.	**a** What are the implications for the company?
2) What I'm going to explain this afternoon are the problems involved in ...	**b** I'm glad to have been offered the opportunity to present ...
3) I'll be developing the three major parts of our project.	**c** Let's go through the possibilities.
4) Let's consider the options.	**d** My presentation will be in three main parts.
5) How will this affect us?	**e** What I'll be proposing in my presentation is my latest invention.

(solutions in the appendix)

Back to Task 1 – Here's the result of our word-watching

Words the chairperson might use

Gentlemen, I'd like to thank you all for your time today.
Thank you very much, gentlemen for sacrificing some of your valuable time to IMM and me. I hope you won't regret it.
As you all know from your pre-conference handouts we'll be having a very unusual meeting today: the presentation of a most exciting piece of hardware.
With this in mind I'd like to welcome Mr Bryan Hemmung and Mr Ronald Bossybitch to K&F's premises. And, of course, IMM himself.
Mr Hemmung, the floor is yours.

Calling a speaker to order

Mr Hemmung, let's not get sidetracked. The issue under discussion is the Intelligent Meet Master.
Could you keep to the point, please?

Thanking the presenter

Well, we'd like to thank you for the information, Mr Hemmung.
I'm sure we all found it very interesting indeed.

Words a presenter might use

Well, to start with, can everybody see? If you can move your chairs in a little.
First, I'd like to show you several OHP sheets with details of IMM's working parts and functions.
I'll use the flipchart for any spontaneous points which might arise.

Structuring the presentation

First, I'd like to show you several OHP sheets with details of IMM's working parts and functions.
Then, in the second part of the meeting, there will be a period for free discussion and question time.
So I'll begin if there are no further questions.

B Task 3: Patch work

consider		implications		main parts
	grateful		issue	
sacrificing		proposing		opportunity
	possibilities		developing	

Can you fit the patches into the right gaps?

I'm .... to have the chance to speak to you.
I'll be .... the three major parts of our project.
Let's .... the options!
What are the .... for the company?
I'm glad to have been offered the .... to present IMM.
Let's go through the ....
My presentation will be in three ....
What I'll be .... in my presentation is my latest invention.
The .... under discussion is the Intelligent Meet Master.
Thank you very much for .... some of your valuable time.

B Task 4: Guided translation

I *(nehme an)* this robot has got a lot of potential.
I've arranged a meeting with a *(möglichen Kunden)*.
Thank you for your *(Unterstützung)*.
So I'll begin if there are no *(weiteren Fragen)*.
Perhaps we could now begin with *(Fragestunde)*.
Mr Hemmung, let's not *(vom Thema abkommen)*.

Time for a smile
Murphy on meetings

A good plan today is better than a perfect plan tomorrow.
A motion[1] to adjourn[2] is always in order.

1 Antrag 2 vertagen

(L) Language box: Use spoken English instead of written English

Most people prepare their presentation in writing. The result is more often than not a written paper and not a presentation. Don't forget that your audience is doing you a favour by listening to you. They want be talked to, so don't read them a paper. Here are some rules you should observe.

- When preparing your presentation, don't copy from catalogues or specifications. They are written English.
- Learning your presentation by heart is almost as bad as reading it to the audience.
- Use your own words and have them checked by one of the native speakers in your company or an English trainer.

Here are a few examples

Avoid written style	**Use spoken English**
A, B, C	*A and B and C*
The Intelligent Meet Master is two metres tall, weighs 200 KGs, has a new generation of brains and the gift of speech.	The Intelligent Meet Master is two metres tall *and* weighs 200 KGs, *and* he has a new generation of brains *and*, most important of all, he has the gift of speech.
third person: he, they	*first or second person: I, you*
Participants of meetings will experience how tiring it is to listen to a presentation that is read by the presenter.	*You* are in a meeting and the presenter doesn't talk to you. He reads his paper. And what happens? *You* doze off after a few minutes. *I* think you all know what *I* mean.
avoid abstract phrases	*call a spade a spade*
The user of the traditional domestic equipment will have encountered disagreeable *failures*.	I suppose *you* know that sort of unpleasant surprise. You buy a *cheap vacuum cleaner* and when you try it at home it starts *blowing instead of sucking*.

(F) The OHP and the seven deadly sins

1) Don't sit – stand!
2) But don't stand in front of the screen.
3) And don't turn your back on the audience.
4) Use a transparent pointer or a biro. Don't point with your hand.
5) Place the pointer on the foil, otherwise the trembling of your hand will be amplified. A small movement becomes a big and hectic movement on the screen.
6) Don't tap on the foil.
7) Don't talk to your foil – talk to the audience.

How to get out of OHP's way

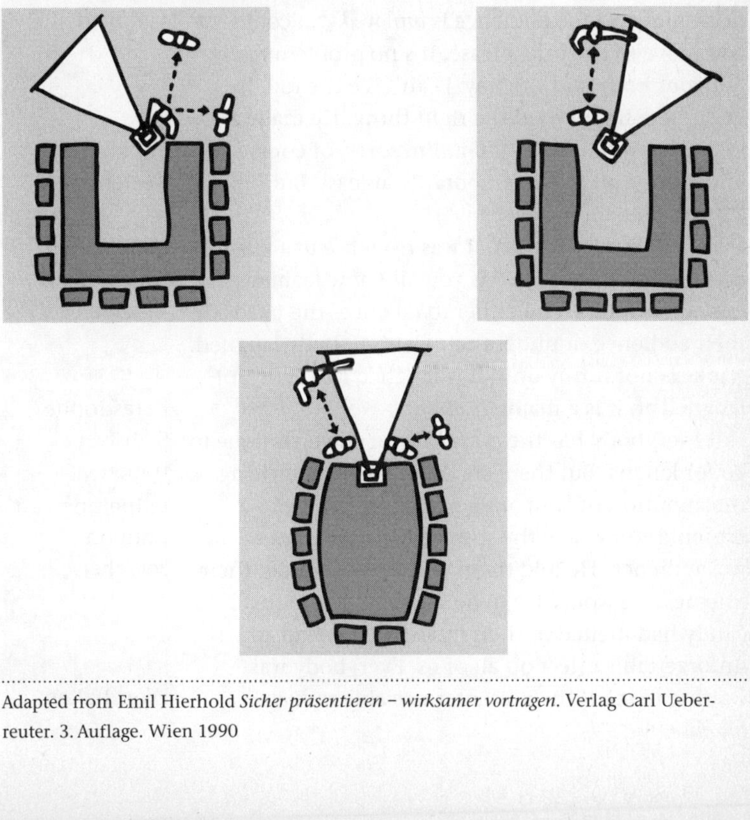

Adapted from Emil Hierhold *Sicher präsentieren – wirksamer vortragen*. Verlag Carl Ueberreuter. 3. Auflage. Wien 1990

(F) The presenter as an entertainer

Presentations are not *lectures*. The professional presenter is sometimes perhaps more of an entertainer than a teacher. Let's go back to Bryan's presentation. He knows the difference between a lecture and a presentation. That's why he started it with what he thought was a *witty* remark. ("I've come to talk to you – you've come to listen to me. If you finish first, please let me know.") Not bad!

But what if it's going badly? For example, when you stand in front of the OHP while you are using it as Bryan did and the audience is *annoyed* ("... could you move to the side, please. It's no problem really but your body's in the way. I can't see the foil.")

Well, here Bryan tried the right thing. He made a joke at *his own expense* ("Oh, I'm sorry, of course. I know I'm a bit big ... temporarily at least. But I'm already on a diet, you know").

However, don't *overdo* it. It was *too much of a muchness* when he went on: "As you all know from experience, presenters tend either to talk over the heads of their audience or under their feet." Nobody laughed. A joke is not funny until it is laughed at. If it is not laughed at, it is a major *disaster*.

Not everybody has the *confidence* or the technique to go for laughs. But there are other ways of catching the attention of your audience. I once *attended* a presentation where the speaker distributed *candy* to the audience. He told them to let it *melt* under their tongues. He would try to be finished before the candy had melted in their mouths. This had an unforgettable effect on all of us. Everybody was waiting to see if the presenter was able to *keep his promise.*

- Vorlesung
- geistreich
- verärgert
- auf eigene Kosten
- übertreiben
- was zuviel ist, ist zuviel
- Katastrophe
- Selbstvertrauen
- teilnehmen an
- Bonbon
- zergehen
- Wort halten

The pastor position and the double American

CONTENTS

Time for a smile: Murphy about opposition and compromise

Never argue[1] with a fool – people might not know the difference.

The compromise will always be more expensive[2] than either of the suggestions[3] it is compromising.

(By the way, Murphy was an optimist)

1 streiten 2 teuer 3 Vorschlag

The pastor position and the double American

(Telephone ringing)

N: Hi, Ron. It's me again. How was Bryan's presentation?

R: He was good. The only thing was his body position and body language. He kept getting in the way of himself. We'll discuss it at tomorrow's meeting.

N: And how did they react to IMM at K&F?

R: I've just had a phone-call with George Kufer. They're going to take IMM on approval. He'll go to their next meeting with a customer.

N: I'm not entirely convinced that this is a good idea. I had a phone-call from that Japanese, Yudeedit. I couldn't really understand what he wanted to say. I think they're trying to detect some hidden flaw. Aren't we taking too many risks if we unleash IMM on an unsuspecting audience?

R: What exactly did Yudeedit say?

N: I couldn't make it out. He was saying IMM was peaceful when the meeting was going on in an orderly way, but he could be strong if people wasted time or did it wrong. I didn't understand too well. Wouldn't it be wiser to wait till we know what Yudeedit means by "IMM could be strong, if ..."?

R: Frankly, I think that is impossible. We've already signed a contract. Yudeedit probably couldn't express himself in English. See you at the meeting then.

At the I.C.S office. Ronald Bossybitch (R), Norbert Kleinstück (N), Amy Fenando (A), Bryan Hemmung (B), Ortrud Gram (O)

R: ... and so let me assure you all that the meeting with Kufer and Faiter went off very successfully.

O: So what is the position concerning the robot?

B: Robotised computer, please Ortrud. He's in another league.

N: Nothing went wrong, did it? I mean that Mr Yudeedit seemed to be worried about something, didn't he?

R: Don't worry, Nob. Everything was under control.

B: I'm afraid it's not as easy as that, Ron. There were some moments when IMM was getting a bit over-authoritarian with one of the owners.

R: He was just a little keen to see things went well. Beginners are often too eager. Now, Bryan, to you!

B: Dear me, I don't like the tone of your voice, Ron. What's up?

R: Now don't get over-sensitive, Bryan. You made a good presentation but there were a few details which need polishing up.

A: Oh Bryan, I thought you told me you'd done a perfect presentation.

O: Perhaps Bryan was blowing his trumpet, Amy.

B: *(angry)* You mean I was blowing my own trumpet, Ortrud.

A: Well, Bryan is a bit of a windbag sometimes. Ha, ha, ha!

B: Well, that's the pot calling the kettle black, isn't it Amy?

N: My god, it's like a kindergarten listening to you arguing. Ron, could you explain what you mean?

R: Certainly. First of all your technique of presenting the information on the OHP. You stood in your own light. It was frustrating. They couldn't see the details.

B: Well, it's easier said than done to remember all those things at the same time. Perhaps I did stand in the way once but ...

R: Well, and I'm afraid your body position was all wrong, too.

B: Oh, I can't accept your comment that my position was all wrong. Perhaps it wasn't perfect but it wasn't so bad.

R: And the other thing I'd like to mention was your body language.

A: Oh, Bryan, has your body started to talk? What language does it speak? Double Dutch? Which parts does your body talk with?

B: I'll just ignore you, Amy. What you all don't seem to realise is how difficult it is to present a product.

R: Yes, I think we know that. But your body language wasn't okay. You didn't seem to be convinced about the product, IMM. You were standing with your hands crossed below your belt. Like a priest.

B: What do you mean 'like a priest'? I'm afraid all these comments are half-baked.

N: It's right, Bryan. There is a body position which is actually called the 'pastor position'.

R: Listen everybody. Thanks to IMM we've got some foils about Bryan's body positions. Ortrud, did you manage to prepare them?

O: No, actually Annette did it.

B: Oh, the ghost herself. I won't ask where she is.

R: No don't! Ortrud, could you put the foils on the OHP?

O: Certainly. Here's the first.

R: Look Bryan. Look at the position of the hands.
That was you. You looked like a virgin on her first date.

B: Well, stone me, Ron! Did I really look like that? Wonders never cease!

A: Oh, that's all very interesting. What do they all mean?

R: Listen, I'll try to explain. Look at number d (see page 139). When you just keep your hands in your pocket, what effect do you think it has on the audience?

O: It makes them think you are not interested in your theme.

B: Well, isn't that interesting? Ronald, why are you standing with both hands in your pocket now? That body position is actually called the 'double American.'

(V) Vocabulary to help you with the text and the exercises

back someone	jemanden unterstützen
be too eager	zu eifrig sein
below the belt	unter die/der Gürtellinie
blow one's own trumpet	sich selbst loben
convinced	überzeugt
detect	entdecken
double Dutch	Kauderwelsch
feasible	machbar
he's in another league.	er ist in einer anderen Klasse
hidden flaw	versteckter Fehler
it went off very successfully	es war sehr erfolgreich
keen; be ~ to do something	scharf sein, etwas zu tun
let me assure you	seien Sie versichert
object to a plan	gegen einen Plan sein
on approval	auf Probe
over-authoritarian	zu autoritär
over-sensitive	überempfindlich
owner	Besitzer
peaceful	friedlich
polish something up	etwas aufpolieren
substantial changes	wesentliche Änderungen

support	unterstützen; Unterstützung
that's the pot calling the kettle black	ein Esel schilt den andern Langohr
unleash someone on	jemanden loslassen auf
unsuspecting	nichtsahnend, ahnungslos
virgin	Jungfrau
windbag	Windbeutel, windiger Bursche
Wonders never cease!	Es gibt noch Wunder!

B Task 1: Word watch

Let's go back to the meeting at ICS. Find nine functions that express disagreement or opposition.

1) How does Nob express his opposition to the contract with K&F? (3)
2) How does Ron disagree with Nob? (1)
3) Bryan doesn't agree with Ron either. How does he express his opposition to Ron's criticism? (5)

(solutions see page 136, Task 3)

B Task 2: Brain test

Tick off the solution which best fits the dialogue.

1) What is the contract about that Ronald has signed with K&F?

- ■ They have bought IMM.
- ■ They will test IMM at one of their customers.
- ■ They will test IMM and buy him if he behaves well.

2) Why does Nob object to this contract?

- ■ IMM is only half-baked.
- ■ He didn't understand what Yudeedit wanted to tell him.
- ■ He suspects that Yudeedit has found something wrong in IMM.

3) What does Ron criticise about Bryan's body language?

- ■ Bryan got in the way of himself.
- ■ He was standing in the 'double American position'.
- ■ He was standing in the 'pastor position'.

Ⓑ Task 3: Mind your manners – Degrees of opposition

These are the speech functions Bryan and Nob used to express their opposition. Put a number into the left box, 1 for the weakest and 9 for the strongest form of opposition.

- ☐ I'm afraid all these comments are half-baked.
- ☐ Frankly, I think that is impossible.
- ☐ I'm afraid it's not as easy as that, Ron.
- ☐ What you all don't seem to realise is how difficult it is to present a product.
- ☐ Aren't we taking too many risks, if we unleash IMM on an unsuspecting audience?
- ☐ It's easier said than done to remember all those things at the same time.
- ☐ I can't accept your comment that my position was all wrong.
- ☐ Wouldn't it be wiser to wait till we know what Yudeedit means by 'IMM could be strong, if ...'?
- ☐ I'm not entirely convinced that this is a good idea.

Time for a smile: Five rules for meetings

Having served on various meetings I have drawn up a list of rules:

1) Never arrive on time: this stamps[1] you as a beginner.
2) Don't say anything until the meeting is half over: this stamps you as wise.
3) Be as vague as possible: this avoids[2] irritating the others[3].
4) When in doubt[4], suggest a subcommittee be appointed[5].
5) Be the first to move for adjournment[6]: this will make you popular[7] – it's what everyone is waiting for.

Harry Chapmas

1 abstempeln 2 vermeiden 3 die anderen verärgern 4 im Zweifelsfall 5 einen Unterausschuß ernennen 6 Vertagung beantragen 7 beliebt

B Task 4: Patch work – How to object

taking		convinced		bit risky
	impossible		as easy as	
accept		easier said		good idea
	wiser		half-baked	

Can you fit the patches into the right gaps?

Frankly, I think that is ....

I'm afraid it's not .... that, Ron.

Isn't it a .... to trust this company?

I'm afraid all these comments are ....

Are you really .... that IMM will behave?

I'm not entirely convinced that this is a ....

It's .... than done to remember all those things.

I can't .... your comment that my position was all wrong.

Wouldn't it be .... to wait till Yudeedit explains what he means?

Aren't we .... too many risks if we sign the contract with K&F?

B Task 5: Word power

Match the functions that are equally tactful, strong or rude

1)	You don't seem to realise that ...	**a**	Are you really convinced that this proposal is going to work?
2)	As it stands, I would not be able to give the project my backing.	**b**	I'm afraid this all only half baked.
3)	This proposal is completely unrealistic.	**c**	Without substantial changes, I cannot give the proposal my support.
4)	Are you sure the proposal is feasible?	**d**	You seem to forget that ...

B Task 6: Scrambled compromises

The opposite of a disagreement is a compromise. Can you repair the functions that announce the readiness for compromise?

a / compromise / let's /strike

....

ready / we / to / you / halfway / are /meet

....

that / compromise / a / reasonable / seems / to be

....

I / be / think / that / perfectly / acceptable /would

....

We / certain / are / prepared concessions / to / make

....

I think / still possible / is / it / a compromise / to strike

L Language box: Question tags (2)

Sometimes questions tags are used to find out if you are in agreement with a person or if a compromise is possible.
(As far as the form of the tag is concerned, please, see chapter 10, page 108.)

I do / I don't	don't you / do you?
I think we could meet halfway,	don't you?
I don't think we should sign the contract,	do you?
We are prepared to make concessions,	aren't you?

Let's	shall we
Let's strike a compromise	shall we?
Let's meet halfway,	shall we?

B Task 7: Guided translation – Revision

I'd like to begin by giving you an *(Überblick über)* the project.
I'll be developing the three *(Hauptteile)* of our project.
If I might *(vorschlagen)* something.
If we could *(zurückkehren)* to the point.
If I could *(zuwenden)* to another subject.
I'm afraid all these projects are *(nicht ganz ausgereift)*.

(F) Focus on body language

a presenter position

b pastor position

c ask me position

d double American position

e keep them at distance position

f James Bond position

Adapted from Emil Hierhold *Sicher präsentieren – wirksamer vortragen*. Verlag Carl Ueberreuter. 3. Auflage. Wien 1990

(F) Meetings in Spain

The Spanish are a proud and *independent* nation.	unabhängig
Theirs is not a meeting culture. Like the torero in the arena the senior executive takes his decisions on his own and uses the meeting to communicate his *instructions.*	Anweisungen
Although most companies have introduced the American philosophy of how to run a company, the idea that a meeting can be used to decide on an action plan, *allocate responsibilities* and coordinate *implementation* is something that is not part of the Spanish mentality.	obwohl / Verantwortung übertragen/Umsetzung
Modern young executives who try to use meetings as a management tool *complain* that they are too long and ineffective. The necessary skills, strategies and the etiquette have still to be learnt.	sich beklagen
Spaniards do not work well in a meeting because they see it as a forum to *defend* their opinion and *obtain* agreement to it rather than arrive at a decision.	verteidigen / erreichen
Unless the chairperson *pulls the subject back to the agenda,* if there is one, it will be rapidly *abandoned.* Consensus is most easily reached by getting everyone to agree with the chairperson rather than with each other. They feel that in the end it is the boss who is *responsible.*	zur Tagesordnung zurückführen/aufgeben / verantwortlich
Britons and Americans who are used to producing a result to which everyone has *contributed* something, and in which everyone will share the *responsibility,* will find this frustrating.	daran gewöhnt / beitragen / Verantwortung

Adapted from John Mole *Mind Your Manners.* Nicholas Brealy Publishing. London 1995

Robot runs riot

CONTENTS

Time for a smile

Amy Fernando has invented the automatic pancake[1]. She puts popcorn in the dough[2] so that it will turn over by itself.

An inventor is a man who has found something more interesting than women.

1 Pfannkuchen 2 Teig

Robot runs riot

N: *(Telephone ringing)* Ron, were you asleep? It's been ringing for hours.

R: No Nob. I was working in the other room. I've got schedules to keep, you know. What's wrong?

N: Today is the moment of truth with IMM.

R: With who? What are you talking about?

N: That damned fool robot. K&F are going to use him to manage a meeting with their customers. Some people from Russia. I can't help worrying. It's given me a stomach problem.

R: You're always worrying. Calm down! Nothing will go wrong!

At K&F, in their conference rooms. Mr Kufer (K), Mr Faiter (F), Mr Zhukov (Z), Mr Plodovski (P) and other managers, IMM (I)

K: Gentlemen, if you are all sitting comfortably then perhaps I could open the meeting. First of all I'd like to welcome Mr Zhukov and Mr Plodovski from the Interior Ministry in Moscow, Russia. They are here to look into the question of buying our distributed software.

I: *(interrupts – metallic voice)* Mr Kufer. It is correct that you make the introduction as you are senior partner. It is not correct that you repeat data about the Russian customer that is already known to all of us. Time-wasting at a meeting!

F: Perhaps I'll take this opportunity to remind you, gentlemen, about IMM, our experimental meeting manager. He should improve the efficiency of our international meetings.

I: *(metallic voice)* I'm afraid there seems to have been a slight misunderstanding. I am not experimental. Moreover, I should not improve efficiency. Allow me to rephrase that: I will improve efficiency. I am efficiency itself. Wouldn't it be better to keep quiet when one cannot introduce accurate data to the meeting?

Z: *(laughing) (in Russian accent)* Ah, Mr Kufer, am I right in assuming that this loud metal man will control our discussion?

K: Well, that was the idea.

I: Again wrong information! It is not an idea. It is a fact. Mr Zhukov, my pronunciation module informs me that we must make some improvements to your accent in English.

Z: Vat do you mean? At me is good accent!
I: Exactly! It must be what and not "vat". Vat is a type of barrel for beer.
K: Oh my god! IMM, can you be quiet?
I: I am not programmed to be quiet. Only to be efficient. And Mr Zhukov, your grammar was out of order. Not "me is good accent" but "I have a good accent".
F: With great respect I think we should return to the reason for our meeting. Now, basically what you said is that you need two thousand pieces of software for use on laptops all over Russia for the collecting of certain types of information which should then be transmitted back to Moscow. Is that correct so far?
(Pause of about 5 seconds. Loud bang like thunder. Everyone's shocked.)
K: What the hell was that?
I: There was a break of five seconds. Mr Zhukov did not answer Mr Kufer's question. This means lack of concentration or even sleeping. Time-wasting! So my software carried out disciplinary action. In the form of simulated thunder. I believe everyone is awake now.
Z: Correct me when I'm wrong, but metal man corrected me?
I: Silence! Language mistakes confuse the meeting. You must say "correct me if I'm wrong, but has the metal man corrected me?" Further I am no man. I am a robotised computer, series twenty-two.
P: Ho, ho, ho! Impossible. Western technology. A world ruled by robots. I think we can close meeting now.
I: Correction! "Close the meeting". Yes, close down is necessary. Too much time-wasting.
K: Now, just a minute. *(Banging and slapping noise)* Ouch!

(V) Vocabulary to help you with the text

assume	annehmen, vermuten
attendee	Anwesende(r)
awake; be ~	wach sein
barrel	Faß
break	Pause
clarification	Klarstellung
clarify	klarstellen, klären

court case	Gerichtsverhandlung
cross purposes; be at ~ ~	aneinander vorbeireden
disciplinary action	disziplinarische Maßnahmen
distribute software	Software vertreiben
improvement	Verbesserung
opportunity; take the ~ to do	die Gelegenheit wahrnehmen
pronounciation	Aussprache
remind someone of something	erinnern; jemanden an etwas ~
run riot	Amok laufen
schedule; keep ~s	Terminpläne einhalten
simulated thunder	simulierter Donner
transmit	übertragen, übermitteln
truth; the moment of ~	die Stunde der Wahrheit

B Task 1: Word watch – How to avoid misunderstandings

Let's go back to the meeting and see what phrases the attendees use to clarify the situation. Can you find them?

1) One way of avoiding them is by repeating what has been said and asking for confirmation or correction (2).

2) Correct the misunderstanding if you are aware of it (1).

3) Rephrase what has been said to see whether you've got it right (2).

(solutions on page 146)

B Task 2: Brain test

Are these statements true (T) or false (F)?

1) K&F have bought IMM. [/]

2) K&F are going to sell IMM to the Russians. [/]

3) K&F want to test IMM at this meeting. [/]

4) Mr Zhukov knew why IMM is present at the meeting. [/]

5) The Russians want to buy 2,000 laptops for the collecting of information for Moscow. [/]

6) The Russians want to buy software for the transmission of data to Moscow. [/]

B Task 3: Patch work – What to say when you feel confused

If you are confused, have a look at the the glossary page 226.

slight		clarify		understood
	cross purposes		clearer	
correct		catch		assuming
	right		follow	

Can you fit the patches into the right gaps?

We seem to be talking at ....

If I've .... you correctly, you're saying that ... .

I'm afraid there seems to have been a .... misunderstanding.

I'm afraid I didn't quite .... what you said about this robot.

If I might explain in more detail it would .... the situation.

Would I be .... in saying that this robot conducts meetings?

Perhaps I should make this .... by saying ... .

I'm afraid we weren't quite able to .... what you were saying.

Am I right in .... that IMM will control our discussion?

What you said is that you need laptops. Is that .... so far?

Food for thought: Advice to managers

1) There are only two kinds of executives who fail[1]: those who listen to nobody, and those who listen to everybody.
2) When confronted by an impossible problem, reduce it to the question "How would Groucho Marx have solved it?"
3) Don't be irreplaceable[2]. If you can't be replaced you can't be promoted[3].
4) Work smarter[4] – not harder.

1 versagen 2 unersetzlich 3 befördern 4 schlauer

Back to Task 1 – How to avoid misunderstandings

How to ask for confirmation or correction

Correct me if I'm wrong, but ...
Am I right in assuming that this loud metal man will control our discussion?

How to clarify a misunderstanding

I'm afraid there seems to have been a slight misunderstanding.

Repeating what has been said

Allow me to rephrase that ... (to make sure that I've understood you correctly).
Now, basically what you said is that you need two thousand pieces of software ... . Is that correct so far?

B Task 4: Word power

Match the functions that are used in the same situation.

1)	Are you saying that ... ?	**a**	I'm afraid I didn't quite follow what you said about ...
2)	If I've understood you correctly, you're saying that ... ?	**b**	Perhaps if I might explain in more detail it would clarify the situation.
3)	I'm afraid we weren't quite able to catch what you were saying.	**c**	When you say ... do you mean ... ?
4)	With respect, that is not what I said.	**d**	Would I be right in saying that ... ?
5)	Perhaps I should make this clearer by saying ...	**e**	We seem to be talking at cross purposes.

You will find more phrases of this kind in the thematic list, page 159.

B Task 5: Guided translation – Revision

(Wenn ich Sie richtig verstanden habe), you're saying that ... .
(Ich fürchte) we weren't quite able *(zu verstehen)* what you were saying.
Perhaps *(sollte ich)* make *(dies klarer)* by saying ...
I'm afraid I didn't *(ganz folgen)* what you said about ...
Perhaps if I *(erläutern dürfte)* in more detail it would *(klären)* the situation.
We seem *(aneinander vorbeizureden)*.

B Task 6: Scrambled clarifications

Can you repair these functions?

am I right / will control our discussion / this metal man / in assuming that?

....

a slight misunderstanding / I'm afraid / to have been / there seems

....

you correctly / allow me / to make sure / that I've understood / to re-phrase that

....

what you said / two thousand pieces of software / now, basically / is that you / need

....

what I / that / is not / said / with respect,

....

purposes / talking / at cross / to be / we seem

....

your robot / I didn't / what you said / I'm afraid / quite follow/ about

....

the situation / if I might / it would clarify / explain / perhaps / in more detail

Time for a smile: How to market a new medicine

Invent an illness.
Mix some vitamins with green colour, give it a latin name (Curabor) and advertise it.
Convince the readers that they have the disease and that it is curable if they use Curabor.

(L) Language box: Comparatives are less direct

Using comparatives (Steigerung) is a polite way of correcting, clarifying and suggesting.

The German way: positive	**The English way: comparative**
To be specific ...	To be *more* specific ...
In simple terms ...	In *simpler* terms ...
Perhaps I should make this clear by saying ...	Perhaps I should make this *clearer* by saying ...
Perhaps if I might explain in detail it would clarify the situation.	Perhaps if I might explain in *more* detail it would clarify the situation.

Let's go back to the dialogue and analyse one of IMM's sentences. He used a comparative when he said to Mr Faiter: "Wouldn't it be *better* to keep quiet when one cannot introduce accurate data ...?"

Let's have a look into IMM's computer brain. How did his Mind-Your-Manners-Module produce this sentence?

Step 1: Unprocessed information
Keep quiet when you you cannot introduce accurate data.

Step 2: A comparative is the first polite element
Better keep quiet if you cannot introduce accurate data.

Step 3: Second polite element: would or might + comparative
It would be better to keep quiet when you cannot introduce accurate data.

Step 4: Third stage of politeness: would or might + comparative + negative question
Wouldn't it be better to keep quiet when you cannot introduce accurate data?

Step 5: Don't be personal: you → one
Wouldn't it be better to keep quiet when one cannot introduce accurate data?

(F) Meetings in the USA

In the United States meetings are *primarily* a communication tool for *imparting* or *gathering* information. The attendee sees it as an *opportunity* to present his proposals, examine the suggestions of his colleagues, *support* or *reject* them. The *object* is not to make a decision but to test the presenter's competence, preparation and *depth* of *knowledge*.
Most decisions will have been lobbied beforehand and will be *approved* at the end of a meeting. A decision is not the result of a *consensus*, in the sense of collective responsibility for a decision *jointly* arrived at, but for a *commitment* to a course of action. If anything goes wrong the participants will not *share* the responsibility. It is their *superior* who alone will be held responsible.
The status of the executive has little to do with *seniority*. It is *determined* by how much power he has. Power is *measured* in how much of the business is under his direct control.
In dealing with colleagues at all *levels* it is important to demonstrate competence and professionalism. Bringing up a problem without a suggested *solution* or without the relevant *data*, in the *expectation* that a solution will be worked out with the participants during the meeting, is a sign of *weakness*. Americans *pursue* their personal and *corporate goals* with frankness, energy and sometimes with aggression. They often lose patience with the *participative* committee cultures of European companies. They may find their European colleagues *lacking in motivation* and commitment.

in erster Linie
mitteilen/sammeln/Gelegenheit
unterstützen/verwerfen/Ziel
Tiefe/Wissen
zustimmen
Übereinkunft
gemeinsam
Verpflichtung
teilen
Vorgesetzter
Dienstalter
bestimmt
messen
Ebene
Lösungsvorschlag/Daten, Fakten/Erwartung/Schwäche
verfolgen/Firmenziele
Mitbestimmungs-
an Motivation fehlen lassen

Adapted from John Mole *Mind Your Manners*. Nicholas Brealy Publishing. London 1995

Was that the end of ICS?

(Telephone ringing)

N: Come on, Ron, where are you? Ah, at last. Ron, it's awful. It's all like I said it would be. We're ruined.

R: Now calm down, Nob! You'll put yourself in hospital with your nerves. What's happened exactly?

N: That metal monster has run riot. It disciplined everybody for every little mistake. It seems to have hit Mr Kufer.

R: My god! Jesus Christ! That damned robot! What on earth got into his metal birdbrain? Let's meet at the office:

At the ICS office. Ronald Bossybitch (R), Norbert Kleinstück (N), Mr Kufer (K)

R: Okay, Nob, we're in trouble. I've got stomach pains.

N: Well, now you know what it's like.

R: We should try to make a compromise with K&F. Let me think a minute.

N: Compromise? That's when two partners move towards each other. After that welded wonder tried to wreck their business there's not much to compromise about.

(Telephone rings)

R: Bossybitch speaking. How can I help you?

K: Help? You can help us by keeping out of the way. You and your whole team and especially that metal murderer, your IMM!

R: Well, I'm sure there's no need to get so excited. We would be perfectly willing to take IMM back and make some improvements.

K: Oh yes! IMM likes improvements. He tried to improve my face with the back of his heavy hand.

R: I guess that was just a reaction in his software.

K: Yes, and then there's the court case.

R: Well, we are certainly prepared to ... I beg your pardon, court case? What do you mean by ...? He's hung up on me.

N: I'll tell you what I think, Ron. This is the end of a beautiful idea.

Chapter 15

All's well that ends well

CONTENTS

The happy end of our story

Time for a smile: Murphy's Law about meetings

1) The length of a meeting is in inverse proportion[1] to its value.
2) Meetings you chair are infinitely better than those you attend[2].
3) Regardless[3] how long a meeting is, all important decisions will be made in the last ten minutes before lunch or quitting time[4].

1 umgekehrt proportional 2 teilnehmen an 3 ganz gleich, egal 4 Zeit zum Gehen

All's well that ends well

At the ICS office, great excitement. Ronald Bossybitch (R), Norbert Kleinstück (N), Amy Fernando (A), Bryan Hemmung (B), Ortrud Gram (O), Mr Zhukov (Z), Mr Plodovski (P), IMM (I)

R: A court case! Nob, I've got stomach-ache with all this trouble.

N: Well, pull yourself together. It's usually me who's feeling sick. Here come the others now. I wonder when the Russians will arrive.

R: Russians? Are they going to prosecute us, as well? *(Sound of people arriving)* Ah, here they are. How do you do, Mr Zhukov and Plodovski?

Z: When I see your face I believe we feel better than you do.

P: Mr Bossybitch, the meeting with K&F was the funniest thing we have ever saw.

N: You mean 'seen'. You have ever seen.

P: Are you also a robot? Perhaps an older version?

N: I'm Bossybitch's partner, actually.

Z: Gentlemen, and you, lovely lady, we could use you in Russia.

A: Oh, gee, thanks!

Z: We want – you see I pronoun it correctly now ...

O: You mean 'pronounce'.

Z: Ah, a female robot. We were sorry about your IMM. We have come to discuss buying IMM and any other IMMs for our country.

R: I can't believe it after his impossible non-democratic behaviour.

Z: Ah, Mr Bossybitch. Democracy is a game only you capitalists can afford. In our country this authoritarian, aggressive metal man will be perfect. He can train soldiers and secret service. But specially our civil servants. We believe IMM is incorruptible. We are willing to buy this product on condition that ...

(Hours later; loud clanking plus a knock at the door)

I: *(metallic)* Good evening. IMM reporting for foreign duty.

R: Ortrud, bring the Champagne and a cup of oil for IMM.

O: It is already done!

(Pop of the cork, champagne is poured into glasses)

R: I raise my glass to the future of ICS and to IMM.

(Murmur, applause, laughter)

(V) Vocabulary to help you with the text

afford	sich leisten
authoritarian	autoritär
behaviour	Benehmen
clank	klirren
court case	Gerichtsverhandlung
foreign duty	Auslandsdienst
incorruptible	unbestechlich
on condition that	unter der Bedingung, daß
pronounce	aussprechen
prosecute	gerichtlich belangen
pull yourself together	reiß' dich zusammen
raise one's glass to	sein Glas erheben auf
report	hier: sich melden
secret service	Geheimdienst
stomach-ache	Bauchweh

Tips for teachers: Group work

The following are suggestions for role-plays or mini-meetings. They are to be used for group work with groups of four or five people. Each background is linked to a chapter with the same number.

Chapter 1

Topics: **Starting up a business in Germany. The pros and cons, the dangers and advantages of being self-employed**

Instructions: Divide the group into two. One side is for starting a business/being self-employed. The other side is against. Use the language of interruption. Check the expressions in chapter one and in the glossary.

Chapter 2

Topics: **Should we make one currency for Europe in1998? Discuss dangers, advantages, consequences for Germany, for Europe.**

Instructions: This time you should role-play a meeting. Choose one chairman and two sides with differing opinions or targets. Take the minutes of the meeting.

Chapter 3

Topics: **1) Show the structure of your company.**
2) Present your main product lines.

Instructions: Divide into groups of four or five. Each group has to make a presentation. Draw a structure for it with introduction etc. Then each group should present it taking a turn each one after the other to show the presentation. Refer to the presentation language guides in chapter three.

Chapter 4

Topics: **1) Students should pay for their studies.**
2) Students should be limited to four years of study.
3) Germany is a wasteland concerning service.

Instructions: Divide into groups of four or five. Have a group discussion about one of the above themes. The language of opinion-giving is in chapter four and the glossary.

Chapter 5

Topics: **My most fascinating holiday, my ideal job etc.**

Instructions: Making a short presentation as an individual. Each member of the group has two or three minutes to think of a theme he should make a presentation on. Use the language of presentation from chapter five and the glossary. Try to use polite language.

Chapter 6

Topics: **The motor car. Does it pay its way?**

Instructions: Divide into two sides. You have to discuss a theme where there will be agreement and disagreement. You will find this type of language in chapter six and in the glossary. Include discussion about pollution, petrol taxes, parking, traffic jams etc., etc.

Chapter 7

Topics: **1) You bang into him/her on the street.**
2) You shout at her/him for leaving the key in the car and locking you both out.
3) You tell your partner off for not locking the door of the apartment etc., etc.

Instructions: Work in pairs! You do something which is rude or hurtful to your partner. Then you should apologise. Think up other typical situations.

Chapter 8

Topics: **The question of the opening times of shops in Germany**

Instructions: In groups of four or five have a meeting. Make it a formal meeting with chairman, teams and minutes. You should build in the language of interruption. You will find some expressions in chapter eight and in the glossary. Alternative: Two teams – for and against opening.

Chapter 9

Instructions: Work in pairs. One partner suggests an idea. The other partner gives reasons for accepting or rejecting it. You can choose your own themes.
Here are some ideas:

Topics:

1) **Reorganise the European Union.**
2) **Put manufacturing out of Germany to save costs.**
3) **German soldiers should take up duty abroad.**
4) **Eliminate smoking from public places, especially restaurants.**
5) **Have speed limits on German motorways.**
6) **Made in Germany. Quality is not so good.**

Chapter 10

Topics:

1) **A hotel booking – misunderstanding about the number of nights.**
2) **Misunderstanding about the time of an appointment (half eight).**

3) Misunderstanding about dates e. g. 02/03/96 (American). – Is it 2nd of March or 3rd of February?

Instructions: Divide into pairs. Think up themes where there could be a potential misunderstanding. The language of misunderstanding and clarification is in chapter ten.

Chapter 11

Topics: **A complete waste of money? The government wants to spend millions of Deutsch-marks on a railway system between Hamburg and Berlin.**

Instructions: Divide into groups of four or five. Choose chairman and teams. The teams are on opposing sides. Use the language functions you have met in the book so far: agreement/disagreement, giving opinions, asking for clarification etc. See glossary for functions.

Chapter 12

Topics: **The necessity of Berlin to be capital of Germany. The cost of the transfer of civil servants and their families.**

Instructions: Divide into groups of four or five. Choose chairman and teams. You are having a debate on TV on a Sunday morning show. Try to build in the language of opinion-giving and interrupting.

Chapter 13

Instructions: Each individual thinks up a theme for a presentation lasting about five minutes. He doesn't present it himself but passes it on to his neighbour who then presents it. Think about your body language (see chapter 13).

Topics:

1) Living in the big city.

2) Compulsory military service.

3) The social network in Germany.
4) My first experience abroad, etc.

Chapter 14

Topics: **The question of civil servants in Germany. Should they be abolished? The advantages and disadvantages of the system including pensions, job security, costs etc.**

Instructions: Divide into groups of four or five. Create a meeting with chairman, minutes etc. Try to build in the language of clarification, avoiding misunderstandings. You will find it in chapter 14 and in the glossary.

Thematic list of 700 speech functions

Redemittel für Vorsitzende

1. Die Eröffnung der Sitzung

Right, shall we get started?	Gut, wollen wir anfangen?
Let's get down to business, shall we?	Kommen wir zur Sache.
Ladies and Gentlemen, I declare the meeting open.	Meine Damen und Herren, ich erkläre die Sitzung für eröffnet.
Ladies and Gentlemen, may I open this meeting now?	Meine Damen und Herren, darf ich die Besprechung nun eröffnen?
Thank you for coming today.	Vielen Dank, daß Sie heute gekommen sind.
I'm happy to welcome all of you to our meeting today on ...	Ich freue mich, Sie heute alle zu unserer Sitzung über ... begrüßen zu dürfen.
I hope we will be able to have a fruitful discussion on ...	Ich hoffe, wir können eine fruchtbare Diskussion über ... führen.
Fred seems to be held up by some act of God again.	Fred scheint wieder einmal durch höhere Gewalt verhindert zu sein.
May I apologise for the fact that Director Block is late?	Darf ich Direktor Blocks Verspätung entschuldigen?

2. Die Tagesordnung

Has everyone received a copy of the agenda?	Haben alle eine Kopie der Tagesordnung erhalten?
Would anybody wish to add another point to our agenda?	Möchte jemand noch einen Punkt auf die Tagesordnung setzen?
I'd like to add an item to the agenda.	Ich möchte der Tagesordnung noch einen Punkt anfügen.
I'd like to put another item on the agenda.	Ich möchte noch einen weiteren Punkt auf die Tagesordnung setzen.
Could we delete item 3 from the agenda?	Könnten wir Punkt 3 der Tagesordnung streichen?

We've got a full agenda!	Wir haben eine umfangreiche Tagesordnung!
The first item on the agenda is ...	Der erste Punkt auf der Tagesordnung ist ...

3. Das Protokoll

Has everybody seen the minutes?	Haben alle das Protokoll eingesehen?
Has everybody got a copy of the minutes of our last meeting?	Haben alle eine Kopie des Protokolls der letzten Besprechung?
Can we take the minutes for read?	Können wir das Protokoll als angenommen betrachten?
Who is going to keep the minutes?	Wer führt das Protokoll?
Bryan has volunteered to keep the minutes, as usual. Thank you, Bryan.	Bryan hat sich wie üblich freiwillig für das Protokoll gemeldet. Danke, Bryan.

4. Ein angenehmes Klima schaffen

I want to begin by thanking Bryan for ...	Ich möchte zuallererst Bryan für ... danken.
I'd like to begin by congratulating Tom on his performance.	Ich möchte zu Beginn Tom zu seiner Leistung gratulieren.
Let's forget the formalities.	Lassen wir die Förmlichkeiten beiseite.
Make yourself at home.	Machen Sie es sich gemütlich.
I appreciate that you are sacrificing an hour of your valuable time.	Ich weiß es zu schätzen, daß Sie uns eine Stunde Ihrer kostbaren Zeit opfern.

5. Art und Anlaß der Sitzung bekanntgeben

The reason for our gathering is ...	Der Grund unseres Beisammenseins ist ...
The purpose of today's meeting is ...	Der Zweck der heutigen Besprechung ist ...
The reason for our coming together is ...	Der Grund für unser Treffen ist ...

As you can see from the agenda ...	Wie Sie der Tagesordnung entnehmen ...
The subject of our meeting is ...	Thema unserer Besprechung ist ...
We've come together today to decide if/whether we should risk ...	Wir sind heute zusammengekommen, um zu entscheiden, ob wir es riskieren sollten ...
I've called you together to have an extraordinary meeting to discuss ...	Ich habe Sie zu einer außerordentlichen Sitzung zusammengerufen, um ... zu besprechen.

6. Einige typische Anlässe

Now, as you all know, we're here to discuss the invention we saw presented.	Nun, wie Sie alle wissen, sind wir hier, um die Erfindung zu besprechen, die uns vorgestellt wurde.
We have to decide on our budget.	Wir müssen unseren Etat beschließen.
Welcome to our weekly production meeting.	Willkommen zu unserer wöchentlichen Produktionsbesprechung.
As you all know we are in a deep recession.	Wie Sie alle wissen, befinden wir uns in einer tiefen Rezession.
We've been having quite a few customer complaints recently.	Wir haben in letzter Zeit eine ganze Reihe Kundenbeschwerden gehabt.
Our R&D department has come up with a new product.	Unsere Forschungsabteilung hat ein neues Produkt entwickelt.

7. Wie man Gastredner behandelt

It is my great pleasure to introduce Mr Yudeedit.	Ich freue mich, Ihnen Herrn Yudeedit vorstellen zu dürfen.
Mr Yudeedit, welcome to ICS in Heidelberg.	Herr Yudeedit, willkommen bei ICS in Heidelberg.
On behalf of the board I extend a hearty welcome to our partners from Japan.	Im Namen des Vorstands heiße ich unsere Partner aus Japan herzlich willkommen.

We have the honour of being addressed by Mr X from Y on the theme of pollution.	Wir haben die Ehre, Herrn X aus Y zum Thema Umweltverschmutzung zu hören.
We're all looking forward to a presentation of what I think is quite an extraordinary little gadget.	Wir freuen uns alle auf die Präsentation eines, wie ich meine, außergewöhnlichen kleinen Geräts.
Mr Yudeedit, will now speak to you about the problem of ...	Herr Yudeedit wird nun zu Ihnen über das Problem ... sprechen.
Mr Yudeedit, over to you.	Herr Yudeedit, bitte sehr.
Mr Yudeedit, the floor is yours.	Herr Yudeedit, Sie haben das Wort.
I'm sure we all found your talk very interesting indeed.	Ich bin sicher, wir haben alle Ihren Vortrag sehr interessant gefunden.
We'd like to thank you for the information, Mr Yudeedit.	Herr Yudeedit, wir möchten Ihnen für die Informationen danken.

8. Den ersten Tagesordnungspunkt angehen

First Mr X is going to give us a short presentation of his latest invention.	Zuerst gibt uns Herr X eine kurze Präsentation seiner neuesten Erfindung.
Let's start with the first item on the agenda (informal).	Lassen Sie uns mit dem ersten Punkt der Tagesordnung beginnen.
The first problem we have to consider is ...	Das erste Problem, das wir zu erörtern haben, ist ...
Perhaps we should first look at ... ?	Vielleicht sollten wir zuerst ... betrachten?
Let us start with a short brainstorm.	Machen wir zuerst ein kurzes Brainstorming.
I should like to begin with a short overview of last quarter's sales figures.	Ich würde gerne mit einem kurzen Überblick über die Verkaufszahlen des letzten Quartals beginnen.
I wish to begin by presenting our new prototype.	Ich möchte Ihnen zu Beginn unseren neuen Prototyp vorstellen.
I'd like to mention briefly ...	Ich würde gerne kurz ... erwähnen.

I'd like to touch upon ...	Ich möchte kurz auf ... eingehen.
First of all, I'd like to make a few remarks concerning ...	Zuallererst würde ich gerne einige Bemerkungen zu ... machen.
I'd like to comment on the problem of ...	Ich würde gerne etwas zu dem Problem des/der ... sagen.
Ladies and gentlemen, let's face it: we've run into serious problems concerning ...	Meine Damen und Herren, sehen wir den Tatsachen ins Auge. Wir haben ernste Schwierigkeiten bei/mit ...
Has anyone anything further they wish to add before we move on to the next item on the agenda?	Hat irgend jemand noch etwas, das er bemerken möchte, bevor wir zum nächsten Punkt übergehen?
And now, my friends, on to the details.	Und nun, meine Freunde, weiter mit den Einzelheiten.

9. Meinungen sammeln

Have you got anything to say,Bob?	Bob, hast du etwas (dazu) zu sagen?
What's your feeling Ron?	Was ist dein Eindruck, Ron?
Tom, I think you know something about the problem.	Tom, ich glaube, du weißt etwas über das Problem.
What are your views on this, Tina?	Was ist deine Ansicht dazu, Tina?
Mr Kelly, would you like to come in here?	Herr Kelly, möchten Sie hierzu etwas sagen?
I wonder if you would like to comment, Ron?	Möchtest du vielleicht etwas dazu beitragen, Ron?
Mrs Gram, would you like to say something about this?	Frau Gram, möchten Sie etwas dazu sagen?
What's your opinion, Tom?	Was ist deine Meinung, Tom?
Would you like to comment, Dan?	Möchtest du dazu Stellung nehmen, Dan?
I'd like Mr Brown to take the floor.	Ich möchte gerne Herrn Brown das Wort erteilen.

Mr Brown, I think you are the expert in this field.	Herr Brown, ich glaube, Sie sind der Experte auf diesem Gebiet.
I think our accountant Dr. Rope would like to make a point.	Ich glaube, unser Buchhalter Dr. Rope möchte dazu Stellung nehmen.
I would like to invite director Block to present his views on ...	Ich würde gerne Herrn Direktor Block bitten, uns seine Meinung über ... zu unterbreiten.

10. Fragen an Teilnehmer weitergeben

Perhaps Mrs Child would care to answer this question?	Vielleicht möchte Frau Child diese Frage beantworten?
I think the production manager is the right man to answer this question.	Ich meine, der Produktionsleiter ist der richtige Mann, um diese Frage zu beantworten.
I'd like to bring in my colleague Tom, who has studied this question in more detail than I have.	Ich würde gerne meinen Kollegen Tom miteinbeziehen, der diese Frage genauer untersucht hat als ich.
I think Dr. Stone is more qualified than I am to deal with this question.	Ich glaube, Dr. Stone kann Ihnen diese Frage besser beantworten als ich.
If I may, I'd like to ask our guest speaker Mr Okono to reply to that.	Wenn Sie gestatten, würde ich gerne unseren Gastredner, Herrn Okono, um eine Antwort bitten.

11. Konferenzdisziplin aufrechterhalten

Let's try to finish by five o'clock.	Versuchen wir, bis 5 Uhr fertig zu sein.
Let's try to keep this meeting short.	Versuchen wir, diese Besprechung kurz zu halten.
Ron, I'm afraid we're moving too far away from the subject.	Ron, ich fürchte, wir kommen zu weit vom Thema ab.
Could you stick to the subject, please?	Könntest du bitte beim Thema bleiben.

Could you keep to the point, Bryan?	Könntest du bei der Sache bleiben, Bryan?
Let's not get side-tracked. The issue under discussion is ...	Wir wollen nicht vom Thema abkommen. Das Problem, das wir diskutieren, ist ...
There seems to be a slight misunderstanding ...	Es scheint da ein kleines Mißverständnis zu herrschen.
I shall have to call you to order, young lady.	Ich muß Sie ermahnen, junge Frau.
We cannot speak all at once.	Wir können nicht alle gleichzeitig sprechen.
I shall have to call you to order, Mr Brain.	Ich muß Sie zur Ordnung rufen, Herr Brain.
I'm afraid your statement is only a subjective interpretation.	Ihre Darstellung ist leider nur eine subjektive Interpretation.
Your contribution is not objective and therefore of little value here.	Ihr Beitrag ist nicht objektiv und deshalb nicht von Belang.
I'm sorry to have to say this, but your comments add nothing to the business of today.	Es tut mir leid, dies sagen zu müssen, aber Ihre Bemerkungen tragen nichts zum heutigen Thema bei.
This will not be recorded in the minutes.	Das kommt nicht ins Protokoll.

12. Probleme vertagen

Perhaps we should leave this for the time being since Tom is ill.	Vielleicht sollten wir dies vorläufig beiseite lassen, da Tom krank ist.
Look, Ron, we may be able to discuss your problem later. Can we take item one now?	Schau, Ron, wir können dein Problem später besprechen. Können wir jetzt mit Punkt 1 beginnen?
I think we should come back to this problem later. We haven't got all the facts yet.	Ich meine, wir sollten später auf dieses Problem zurückkommen. Wir verfügen noch nicht über alle Fakten.
Perhaps we can discuss that at a later date.	Wir können das vielleicht zu einem späteren Zeitpunkt besprechen.

Let's worry about that later. At the moment we have more urgent problems.	Kümmern wir uns später darum. Im Moment haben wir dringendere Probleme.
I suggest we leave this matter until our next meeting.	Ich schlage vor, wir heben uns diese Angelegenheit für die nächste Besprechung auf.
If nobody has any objections, I propose we postpone this item till we get the latest figures.	Wenn niemand Einwände erhebt, schlage ich vor, wir verschieben diesen Punkt, bis wir die neuesten Zahlen haben.
If you agree, I propose we defer this matter until we have more information at our disposal.	Wenn Sie einverstanden sind, verschieben wir diese Sache, bis uns mehr Informationen zur Verfügung stehen.

13. Ergebnisse zusammenfassen und sichern

In short, the main points that have been made are ...	Um es kurz zu machen, die wichtigsten Punkte/Argumente sind ...
If I may just go over the main points which have been raised so far ...	Wenn ich kurz die wichtigsten Argumente, die vorgebracht wurden, noch einmal nennen darf ...
Well, if I could just sum up the discussion ...	Wenn ich nun unsere Diskussion zusammenfassen darf ...
To summarise I think we are in agreement on ...	Ich glaube, ich kann zusammenfassend sagen, daß wir uns über ... einig sind.
To sum up, it seems that we have a consensus.	Um es zusammenzufassen, es scheint Einigkeit zu herrschen.

14. Der letzte Punkt der Tagesordnung: Sonstiges

Any Other Business (A.O.B.)	Sonstiges
Is there any other business?	Gibt es sonst noch etwas?
Any further points?	Noch irgendwelche Punkte?

Is there anything else to discuss?	Gibt es sonst noch etwas zu besprechen?
Has anyone anything further they wish to discuss?	Hat jemand noch etwas, das wir besprechen sollten?
Any further points before we bring this meeting to an end?	Noch irgendwelche Punkte, bevor wir die Sitzung schließen?

15. Eine Abstimmung durchführen

Let's have a vote on this.	Stimmen wir darüber ab.
Let's put it to the vote.	Stimmen wir darüber ab.
Could we move to a vote on this?	Könnten wir zur Abstimmung schreiten?
Could we take a vote on it?	Könnten wir dies zur Abstimmung bringen?
Perhaps we should take a formal vote on this.	Vielleicht sollten wir in aller Form darüber abstimmen.
In the event of a tie I would like to remind you that I have the casting vote.	Ich möchte Sie daran erinnern, daß im Falle von Stimmengleichheit meine Stimme den Ausschlag gibt.
Can I ask for a show of hands?	Darf ich um Handzeichen bitten?
Those in favour raise their hands.	Wer dafür ist, möge die Hand heben.
Those in favour say 'Aye'.	Wer dafür ist, stimme mit 'Ja'.
Those for the motion, please?	Wer ist dafür?
Those against?	Wer ist dagegen?
Any abstentions?	Wer enthält sich der Stimme?
The motion is carried by seven votes to four.	Der Antrag ist mit sieben zu vier Stimmen angenommen.
The motion is rejected by eight votes to three.	Der Antrag ist mit acht zu drei Stimmen abgelehnt.
The motion is carried unanimously.	Der Antrag ist einstimmig angenommen.

16. Einigkeit und Harmonie betonen

Are we all agreed on that?	Sind wir uns darüber alle einig?
Can I take it everyone is in favour?	Darf ich annehmen, daß alle dafür sind?
Well, we're broadly in agreement on that.	Wir sind uns also weitgehend darüber einig.
Well, it looks as if we have a consensus.	Es scheint so, als hätten wir Übereinstimmung erzielt.
I think we have had a most fruitful discussion.	Ich finde, wir haben eine sehr fruchtbare Diskussion geführt.
I think we've come to the conclusion that ...	Ich glaube, wir sind zu dem Schluß gekommen, daß ...
We seem to have reached a mutual understanding.	Mir scheint, wir haben ein beiderseitiges Einvernehmen erzielt.
We obviously have a firm basis on which to proceed.	Wir haben offenbar eine sichere Grundlage, auf der wir weiterarbeiten können.
We seem to have arrived at a workable solution to the problem.	Wir scheinen eine praktikable Lösung für das Problem gefunden zu haben.

17. Die Sitzung beenden

Could we adjourn the meeting to Monday?	Könnten wir die Besprechung auf Montag vertagen?
That's all for today. Thank you.	Das ist alles für heute. Vielen Dank.
I'd like to call it a day now.	Ich würde für heute gerne Feierabend machen.
Let's call it a day!	Feierabend für heute!
Well, I think we've covered everything.	Gut, ich glaube, wir haben alles berücksichtigt.
Well, I think we've discussed everything.	Nun, ich glaube, wir haben alles besprochen.

If nobody has anything to add I'd like to draw the meeting to an end.	Wenn niemand mehr etwas zu sagen hat, würde ich die Besprechung gerne schließen.
I'd now like to bring this meeting to an end by saying ...	Ich würde die Sitzung gerne mit den Worten schließen: ...
That concludes our business for today. Thank you.	Damit wäre unser Geschäft für heute erledigt. Vielen Dank.
I declare the meeting closed. Thank you, Ladies and Gentlemen.	Ich erkläre die Sitzung für geschlossen. Vielen Dank, meine Damen und Herren.

Meinungen äußern

1. Vorsichtige Meinungsäußerung

Well, of course I'm no expert on ... but I thought ...	Nun, ich bin natürlich kein Fachmann für ... , aber ich dachte ...
I, for my part, would say that ...	Nun, was mich angeht, so würde ich sagen ...
As far as I'm able to judge ...	Soweit ich dies beurteilen kann ...
It seems to me that ...	Mir scheint, daß ...
It appears to me as if ...	Mir scheint, als ob ...
It would seem to me that ...	Ich würde meinen, daß ...
I tend to think that ...	Ich neige zu der Ansicht, daß ...
I think it would be fair to say ...	Ich glaube, man könnte sagen, daß ...
It looks as if ...	Es scheint so zu sein, daß ...

2. Sagen, was man denkt

If you ask me ...	Wenn Sie mich fragen ...
I'd say that ...	Ich würde sagen, daß ...
I presume ...	Ich nehme an, daß ...

I reckon that ...	Ich schätze, daß ...
If you want to know my opinion, I'd say that ...	Wenn Sie meine Meinung wissen wollen, ich würde sagen, daß ...
I feel that .../I think that ...	Ich meine, daß ...
I believe that ...	Ich glaube, daß ...
In my view/In my opinion ...	Meiner Meinung nach ...
In my eyes ...	In meinen Augen ...
It's my opinion that ...	Es ist meine Meinung, daß ...
As I see it ...	Wie ich es/die Sache sehe ...
As far as I'm concerned, I think that ...	Was mich anbelangt, so glaube ich, daß ...
From my point of view things are different.	Von meinem Standpunkt aus gesehen, liegen die Dinge anders.
Let me put it this way ...	Lassen Sie es mich einmal so sagen ...

3. Seine Überzeugung zum Ausdruck bringen

I'm quite sure that ...	Ich bin ziemlich sicher, daß ...
I'm certain that ...	Ich bin sicher, daß ...
I'm convinced that ...	Ich bin überzeugt, daß ...
It is my conviction, that ...	Es ist meine Überzeugung, daß ...
I'm absolutely certain that ...	Ich bin absolut sicher, daß ...
It's quite /absolutely clear that ...	Es ist völlig klar, daß ...
It stands to reason that ...	Es liegt auf der Hand, daß ...
It's my belief/conviction that ...	Es ist meine Überzeugung, daß ...
It's my firm belief that ...	Es ist meine feste Überzeugung, daß ...
I firmly believe that ...	Ich bin fest davon überzeugt, daß ...
I sincerely believe that	Es ist meine ehrliche Überzeugung, daß ...

It's my considered opinion that ...	Es ist meine wohlüberlegte Meinung, daß ...
You can count/bet on that!	Darauf können Sie Gift nehmen!

4. Meinungen anderer einholen

What do you think of ... ?	Was hältst du von ... ?
What's your opinion of ...?	Was ist deine Meinung zu ... ?
What's your view on ... ?	Wie ist deine Meinung zu ... ?
What's your feeling, Bob?	Was meinst du dazu, Bob?
What is your point of view?	Was ist dein Standpunkt?
What's your position on ...?	Wie stehst du zu ...?
How do you see the problem?	Wie sehen Sie das Problem?
I'd like to hear your views on ...	Ich würde gerne eure Meinungen zu ... hören.
I wonder if you'd like to comment, Tina?	Möchtest du vielleicht etwas dazu sagen, Tina?
May I ask for reactions to Susan's presentation?	Darf ich um Reaktionen zu Susans Präsentation bitten?
And where exactly do you stand on this issue, Dr. Brain?	Und wo stehen Sie in dieser Frage, Dr. Brain?
I'd like to ask Professor Dosch to give us his view.	Ich würde gerne Herrn Professor Dosch bitten, uns seine Meinung zu sagen.
Has anybody thought of the legal aspect of the project?	Hat jemand an die rechtliche Seite des Projekts gedacht?
John, I think you are the specialist in legal matters.	John, ich glaube du bist der Spezialist in juristischen Dingen.
Would you like to comment on this, Tom?	Möchtest du dich dazu äußern, Tom?

Argumente gekonnt vorbringen

1. Überblick geben und klar strukturieren	
There are three problems that should be solved today.	Drei Probleme sollten heute gelöst werden.
There are three decisions to be taken today.	Heute müssen drei Entscheidungen gefällt werden.
There are three points I'd like to make.	Ich möchte drei Argumente vorbringen.
The most important issue seems to me to be ...	Die wichtigste Frage scheint mir ... zu sein.
There are two points to be borne in mind.	Zwei Dinge müssen wir im Auge behalten.
First of all, we must bear in mind ...	Zuallererst dürfen wir nicht vergessen, daß ...
Firstly, ... Secondly, ...	Erstens ... Zweitens ...
First, ... Second, ... Third, ...	Erstens ... Zweitens ... Drittens ...
To begin with, let me say this: ...	Lassen Sie mich eingangs folgendes sagen: ...

2. Ein neues Argument einführen	
Let's now turn to the problem of pollution.	Wir wollen uns nun dem Problem der Umweltverschmutzung zuwenden.
The next question I would like to focus on is ...	Die nächste Frage, auf die ich mich konzentrieren möchte, ist ...
The next issue I would like to concentrate on is ...	Die nächste Frage, auf die ich mich konzentrieren möchte, ist ...
Turning to the issue of security ...	Wenn wir uns dem Sicherheitsproblem zuwenden ...
To turn to another subject: ...	Um auf ein anderes Thema zu sprechen zu kommen: ...

3. Zusatzargumente vorbringen

Moreover ...	Darüber hinaus ...
Furthermore ...	Ferner ...
In addition ...	Hinzu kommt ...
And, more important, ...	Und, was noch wichtiger ist, ...
I'd like to add that ...	Ich würde gerne hinzufügen, daß ...
I might also add that ...	Ich könnte noch anführen, daß ...
If I might just add something here ...	Wenn ich an dieser Stelle noch etwas hinzufügen dürfte ...
I wish to add two sentences to the discussion ...	Ich möchte zu der Diskussion noch zwei Sätze sagen.
Here one might add that ...	Man könnte an dieser Stelle hinzufügen, daß ...
Not only X, but also Y.	Nicht nur X, sondern auch Y.
As well as X, there is also Y.	Ebenso wie X, ist da noch Y.
And let us not forget the following: ...	Und lassen Sie uns folgendes nicht vergessen: ...

4. Argumente anschaulich machen

To illustrate this point I'd like to show you the model of ...	Um diesen Punkt zu veranschaulichen, würde ich Ihnen gerne das Modell von ... zeigen.
Let me give you a few examples.	Lassen Sie mich Ihnen ein paar Beispiele geben.
What does that mean in practice?	Was bedeutet das in der Praxis?
A typical case of this sort is ...	Ein typischer Fall dieser Art ist ...
A case in point is ...	Ein typisches Beispiel ist ...
Could you help us with an example of what you mean?	Könnten Sie uns ein Beispiel geben, damit wir sehen, was Sie meinen.

5. Objektiv sein und beide Seiten betrachten

Let's consider the options.	Betrachten wir die Alternativen.
Let's go through the possibilities.	Gehen wir die Möglichkeiten durch.
On the one hand ..., on the other hand ...	Einerseits ..., andererseits ...
Although we mustn't forget that ...	Obwohl wir nicht vergessen dürfen, daß ...
Whereas we must admit that...	Wobei wir zugeben müssen, daß ...
Inspite of the price I still think that ...	Trotz des Preises glaube ich doch, daß ...
Despite the fact that ..., I think ...	Trotz der Tatsache, daß ..., meine ich ...
We have to weigh the options before we can take a decision.	Wir müssen die Alternativen abwägen, bevor wir eine Entscheidung fällen können.

6. Die Diskussion in die gewünschte Richtung lenken

Shouldn't we rather turn to the question of ... ?	Sollten wir uns nicht besser der Frage des/der ... zuwenden?
I think it might be a good idea if we discussed the more important question of ... ?	Ich glaube, es wäre gut, wenn wir uns der wichtigeren Frage des ... zuwenden würden?
I'm afraid we're losing sight of the main point. The problem is ..., isn't it?	Ich fürchte, wir verlieren die Hauptsache aus den Augen. Das Problem ist doch ...
I'm afraid this isn't really relevant to our discussion. The question is whether we ...	Ich fürchte, dies ist für unsere Diskussion nicht von Bedeutung. Die Frage ist doch, ob wir ...
I think we should turn our attention to the more important issue of X.	Ich meine, wir sollten unsere Aufmerksamkeit dem wichtigeren Problem X zuwenden.

I, for my part, think the main advantage of ... is ...	Was mich betrifft, so glaube ich, der größte Vorteil von ... ist ...
I'd rather turn to the next point on the agenda.	Ich würde lieber zum nächsten Tagesordnungspunkt übergehen.
We may be able to deal with your problem later.	Wir können uns mit deinem Problem später befassen.
I'd prefer to move on to item two.	Ich würde lieber mit Punkt zwei weitermachen.

7. Argumente verallgemeinern

In general ...	Im allgemeinen ...
This is the overall situation.	So stellt sich die Situation insgesamt dar.
Generally speaking ...	Allgemein gesprochen ...
Broadly speaking ...	Allgemein gesprochen ...
All in all I think the new project will be a success.	Alles in allem glaube ich, daß das neue Projekt ein Erfolg sein wird.
By and large ...	Im großen und ganzen ...
Looking at it from a distance ...	Aus der Distanz betrachtet ...
Ignoring the details, it boils down to ...	Wenn wir einmal von den Details absehen, so läuft es auf ... hinaus.
All things considered, I'm sure this is the right decision.	Unter Berücksichtigung aller Aspekte bin ich sicher, daß dies die richtige Entscheidung ist.
On the whole we can be satisfied with the results.	Insgesamt können wir mit den Ergebnissen zufrieden sein.

8. Seine Argumentation zum Abschluß bringen

Let me conclude by saying ...	Lassen Sie mich mit den Worten schließen ...
Let me conclude by emphasising one thing: ...	Lassen Sie mich zum Abschluß eines betonen: ...

Let me conclude by stressing the fact that ...	Lassen Sie mich zum Abschluß die Tatsache hervorheben, daß ...
I'd like to conclude by stating that ...	Ich möchte mit der Feststellung schließen, daß ...
In conclusion I'd like to say ...	Zum Schluß möchte ich sagen, daß ...
I'd like to conclude my comments by quoting Shakespeare.	Ich möchte meine Ausführungen mit einem Shakespeare-Zitat schließen.

Einen Sprecher unterbrechen

1. Unterbrechen, um zu widersprechen

Hang on.	Moment mal.
Sorry to butt in, but ...	Entschuldigen Sie, wenn ich Ihnen ins Wort falle, aber ...
Sorry to break in, but ...	Tut mir leid, wenn ich Sie unterbreche, aber ...
I don't want to interrupt you, but ...	Ich möchte Sie nicht unterbrechen, aber ...
I'm sorry to interrupt you here, but ...	Entschuldigen Sie, wenn ich Sie hier unterbreche, aber ...
Excuse me, could I just break in a moment here ...?	Entschuldigen Sie, aber könnte ich kurz etwas dazu sagen?
May I interrupt you for a moment?	Darf ich Sie für einen Augenblick unterbrechen?
If I may just interrupt you for a moment, I'd like to remind you that ...	Wenn ich Sie kurz unterbrechen dürfte. Ich würde Sie gerne daran erinnern, daß ...
Excuse me, may I ask a question?	Entschuldigen Sie, darf ich Ihnen eine Frage stellen?
Pardon me for interrupting, but is this really relevant?	Ich bitte um Entschuldigung, wenn ich Sie unterbreche, aber gehört das wirklich zur Sache?

Excuse me, but may I play the devil's advocate for a moment?	Verzeihen Sie, aber darf ich für einen Augenblick des Teufels Advokaten spielen?

2. Unterbrechen, um einen Beitrag zu machen

If I can just make a point here ...	Wenn ich dazu gerade etwas bemerken darf ...
If I could just come in here ...	Wenn ich dazu gerade etwas sagen dürfte ...
May I come in at this point?	Darf ich Sie kurz unterbrechen?
If I might just add one more argument in favour of ...	Wenn ich noch ein weiteres Argument zugunsten von ... beisteuern dürfte ...
If I just might say a few words about ...	Wenn ich vielleicht ein paar Worte über/zu ... sagen dürfte.
If no one objects, I'd like to say a word about ...	Wenn niemand etwas dagegen hat, würde ich gerne etwas zu ... sagen.
Excuse me, but before we go any further, could I point out that ...?	Entschuldigen Sie bitte, aber bevor wir fortfahren, dürfte ich darauf hinweisen, daß ... ?
Excuse me, but before we move on to the next item, I'd like to add that ...	Entschuldigen Sie, aber bevor wir zum nächsten Punkt übergehen, würde ich gerne ergänzend bemerken, daß ...
I'd like to add something here, if I may.	Ich würde gerne dazu etwas bemerken, wenn Sie erlauben.
Excuse me, but I think it's important to add that ...	Entschuldigen Sie, aber ich glaube es ist wichtig hinzuzufügen, daß ...
I wonder if I might comment upon your last argument?	Dürfte ich wohl etwas zu Ihrem letzten Argument bemerken?
Excuse me, but may I just draw your attention to the fact that ...	Entschuldigen Sie, aber darf ich Ihre Aufmerksamkeit auf die Tatsache lenken, daß ...

3. Wie man nach der Unterbrechung fortfährt

If I could just continue. I'll answer your question in a minute.	Wenn ich fortfahren dürfte. Ich werde Ihre Frage gleich beantworten.
Thank you for your comment.	Vielen Dank für Ihre Bemerkung.
You took the words right out of my mouth.	Sie nehmen mir die Worte aus dem Mund.
As I was saying ...	Wie gesagt, ...
Coming back to what I was trying to explain ...	Um auf das zurückzukommen, was ich zu erklären versuchte ...
Going back to what I was saying ...	Zurück zu dem, was ich sagen wollte ...
To go back to what I was saying ...	Um auf das zurückzukommen, was ich sagen wollte ...
To return to my subject ...	Um zu meinem Thema zurückzukehren ...
Perhaps I could resume my presentation.	Vielleicht dürfte ich mit meiner Präsentation fortfahren.
If we could return to the issue.	Könnten wir wieder zur Sache kommen?
If I might just go back to the point I was making ...	Wenn ich meinen Gedanken wiederaufnehmen dürfte ...
If I could now turn to another question ...	Wenn ich mich nun einer anderen Frage zuwenden dürfte ...
Thank you for your question which leads us back to the subject.	Vielen Dank für Ihre Frage, die uns wieder zum Thema zurückführt.
Thank you for having cleared up a misunderstanding. This brings me to the next point I was going to make.	Vielen Dank, daß Sie ein Mißverständnis aufgeklärt haben. Das bringt mich zu dem nächsten Punkt, auf den ich eingehen wollte.

4. Wie man Unterbrechungen ablehnt

If I could just continue ...	Wenn ich gerade fortfahren dürfte ...
If I might just finish my sentence ...	Wenn ich meinen Satz beenden dürfte ...
Perhaps we could return to your question later on.	Wir könnten auf Ihre Frage vielleicht später eingehen.
With respect, I should like to add only this ...	Entschuldigen Sie, aber ich möchte gerne noch folgendes sagen: ...
With your permission, I'd rather finish what I was saying.	Mit Ihrer Erlaubnis würde ich gerne meinen Satz zu Ende bringen.
If you would allow me to round off my argumentation.	Wenn Sie gestatten, würde ich meine Ausführungen gerne abschließen.
If you would be so kind as to let me finish. There's enough time to answer all your questions later on.	Wenn Sie so freundlich wären, mich ausreden zu lassen. Wir haben genug Zeit, um alle Ihre Fragen später zu beantworten.

5. Wie man Unterbrechungen von vornherein ausschließt

Please let me finish my presentation. Afterwards I'll answer any questions you might still have.	Lassen Sie mich meine Präsentation bitte zu Ende führen. Anschließend werde ich alle Fragen, die Sie dann noch haben, beantworten.
I'd just like to give you two examples. Then I'll answer your questions.	Ich möchte Ihnen nur noch zwei Beispiele geben. Dann gehe ich auf Ihre Fragen ein.
Very briefly, just one more sentence that might answer your question.	Ganz kurz nur noch einen Satz, der vielleicht Ihre Frage beantwortet.
There are two points I'd like to make, before I answer your questions.	Ich möchte zwei Punkte betonen, bevor ich Ihre Fragen beantworte.
In order to fully understand the situation, you should know this: ...	Um die Situation voll und ganz zu verstehen, müssen Sie folgendes wissen: ...

First I would like to reply to our guest, Mr Brain, and then I'll come back your objection, Mr Dumbar.	Zuerst möchte ich die Frage unseres Gastes, Herrn Brain, beantworten, anschließend komme ich auf Ihren Einwand zurück, Herr Dumbar.

Gegenargumente und Widerspruch

1. Vorsichtig und taktvoll widersprechen

Isn't it a bit risky to trust this company?	Ist es nicht ein bißchen gewagt, dieser Firma zu trauen?
Is it safe to give this client such a huge loan?	Ist es sicher, diesem Kunden einen so hohen Kredit zu geben?
Aren't we taking too many risks if we ...?	Gehen wir nicht zu viele Risiken ein, wenn wir ...?
Do you think that the project is really worthwhile?	Glauben Sie, daß sich das Projekt wirklich lohnt?
I can see certain problems in adopting this strategy.	Ich sehe da gewisse Probleme, wenn wir dieser Strategie folgen.
I can see some difficulties lying ahead, if we adopt this plan.	Ich sehe da einige Schwierigkeiten auf uns zukommen, wenn wir diesen Plan annehmen.
Are you sure the proposal is feasible?	Sind Sie sicher, daß dieser Vorschlag zu verwirklichen ist?
I'm not entirely convinced that this is a realistic proposal.	Ich bin nicht völlig überzeugt, daß dies ein realistischer Vorschlag ist.
Are you really convinced that this plan is going to work?	Sind Sie wirklich überzeugt, daß dieser Plan klappen wird?
On the face of it, this seems quite a good suggestion, but ...	Auf den ersten Blick scheint dies ein ganz guter Vorschlag zu sein, aber ...
Wouldn't it be wiser to sleep on it?	Wäre es nicht besser, dies zu überschlafen?
Would it be reasonable to ...?	Wäre es vernünftig, wenn wir ...?

Wouldn't it be wiser to ...?	Wäre es nicht klüger, wenn wir ...?
I don't think it's quite as simple as that.	Ich glaube nicht, daß das so einfach ist.
I'm afraid it is easier said than done.	Ich fürchte, dies ist leichter gesagt als getan.
I'm afraid it's not as easy as that.	Ich fürchte, es ist nicht so leicht, wie es aussieht.
I'm afraid I can't give my wholehearted support to this proposal.	Ich kann diesem Vorschlag leider nicht ganzen Herzens unterstützen.
That's all very well, but ...	Das ist alles schön und gut, aber ...
You don't seem to realise that ...	Es scheint Ihnen nicht klar zu sein, daß ...
You seem to forget that ...	Sie scheinen zu vergessen, daß ...
Let me try to pick a few holes in your argument.	Lassen Sie mich versuchen, Ihre Argumente zu entkräften.

2. Ungeschminkte Ablehnung

I'm opposed to this proposal, because ...	Ich bin gegen diesen Vorschlag, weil ...
I'm afraid I can't support/back the proposal.	Ich kann diesen Vorschlag leider nicht unterstützen.
The plan may be good on paper, but it will never work in practice.	Der Plan mag sich auf dem Papier ganz gut ausnehmen, aber in der Praxis ist er nicht durchführbar.
As it stands, I would not be able to give the project my backing.	So wie die Dinge liegen, könnte ich das Projekt nicht unterstützen.
Without substantial changes I cannot give the proposal my support.	Ohne wesentliche Änderungen kann ich dem Vorschlag nicht zustimmen.

3. Starken Widerspruch erheben

Your arguments don't hold water.	Ihre Argumente sind nicht stichhaltig.
I'm totally/completely/wholly/ definitely opposed to the motion.	Ich bin absolut gegen diesen Antrag.

Frankly, I think that is impossible.	Offen gesagt, ich halte das für unmöglich.
This proposal is completely unrealistic.	Dieser Vorschlag ist völlig unrealistisch.
I'm afraid this proposal leaves a great deal to be desired.	Dieser Vorschlag läßt leider viel zu wünschen übrig.
I'm afraid this is all only half-baked.	Ich fürchte, dies ist alles etwas unausgegoren.

Unklarheiten klären, Mißverständnisse vermeiden

1. Überprüfen, ob man richtig verstanden hat

Basically, what you are saying is ...	Was Sie sagen, ist im Grunde ...
Are you saying that ... ?	Wollen Sie sagen, daß ...?
When you say ..., do you mean ...?	Wenn Sie sagen ..., meinen Sie damit ...?
If I've understood you correctly, you're saying that ... ?	Wenn ich Sie recht verstanden habe, sagen Sie, daß ...?
Would I be right in saying that ...?	Wäre es richtig, wenn ich sage, daß ...?
Am I correct in assuming that ...?	Gehe ich recht in der Annahme, daß ...?
Correct me if I'm wrong, but ...	Korrigieren Sie mich, wenn ich mich irre, aber ...

2. Wie man eine Frage einleitet

May I ask how/if/why/what ...?	Darf ich fragen ob/warum/was ...?
Would you mind if I asked ...?	Gestatten Sie die Frage ...?
Would you mind me asking a question?	Gestatten Sie, daß ich Ihnen eine Frage stelle?
I wonder if I could ask you if ...?	Darf ich Sie fragen, ob ...?

3. Um Wiederholung bitten

I'm afraid I don't understand what you mean.	Ich fürchte, ich verstehe nicht ganz, was Sie meinen.
It depends what you mean by that.	Es kommt darauf an, was Sie darunter verstehen.
I'm afraid we weren't quite able to catch what you were saying.	Leider konnten wir akustisch nicht verstehen, was Sie sagten.
I'm afraid I didn't quite follow what you said about ...	Ich konnte Ihnen leider nicht ganz folgen bei dem, was Sie über ... sagten.
I'm afraid I'm not quite sure what you mean by that.	Ich fürchte, mir ist nicht ganz klar, was Sie damit meinen.
I'm afraid I didn't get your last point. Could you go over it again please?	Ich habe Ihren letzten Punkt leider nicht ganz verstanden. Könnten Sie das noch einmal wiederholen?
Could we see the last transparency again, please?	Könnten wir bitte die letzte Folie noch einmal sehen?

4. Auf Fragen eingehen

That's a very interesting question.	Das ist eine sehr interessante Frage.
That's a very complex problem.	Das ist ein sehr schwieriges Problem.
That's a difficult question to answer.	Diese Frage ist nicht einfach zu beantworten.
I'm glad you asked this question.	Ich freue mich, daß Sie diese Frage gestellt haben.
You've raised an important point there.	Sie haben da einen wichtigen Punkt angesprochen.

5. Fragen ausweichen

I'm afraid there isn't enough time to go into every detail.	Ich fürchte, wir haben nicht genug Zeit, um auf jedes Detail einzugehen.
I'm afraid there isn't enough time to consider all the aspects of the problem.	Ich fürchte, es ist nicht genug Zeit, um alle Aspekte des Problems zu behandeln.

I think we can leave this problem aside for the moment. The real question is ...	Ich meine, wir können dieses Problem im Augenblick beiseite lassen. Die eigentliche Frage ist ...
Well, it's rather difficult to say at present ...	Nun, es ist zum jetzigen Zeitpunkt schwer zu sagen ...
I'm afraid I don't have enough information at my disposal to answer that.	Mir stehen leider nicht genügend Informationen zur Verfügung, um dies zu beantworten.
I must admit that I don't know the answer, if answer there is.	Ich muß zugeben, ich habe keine Antwort darauf, wenn es überhaupt eine geben sollte.

6. Um Zusatzinformation bitten

Could you be a little more precise/specific/explicit?	Könnten Sie sich etwas genauer ausdrücken?
Could you expand on that?	Könnten Sie das noch etwas weiter ausführen?
Would you care to elaborate on that?	Würden Sie dies bitte etwas ausführlicher beschreiben?
Could you give us some more details about ...?	Könnten Sie uns noch mehr Einzelheiten über ... geben?
Could you explain in a little more detail?	Könnten Sie etwas mehr in die Einzelheiten gehen?
Could you give us some examples to make this clearer?	Könnten Sie uns ein paar Beispiele nennen, um das zu verdeutlichen?

7. Mißverständnisse deutlich machen

We seem to be talking at cross purposes.	Wir scheinen aneinander vorbeizureden.
I'm afraid you've misunderstood me.	Ich fürchte, Sie haben mich mißverstanden.
I'm afraid there seems to have been a slight misunderstanding.	Ich fürchte, da besteht ein kleines Mißverständnis.

With respect, that is not what I said.	Entschuldigen Sie, aber das ist nicht das, was ich gesagt habe.
That isn't quite what I meant.	Das ist nicht ganz das, was ich meinte.
This isn't exactly what I was trying to get across.	Das ist nicht genau das, was ich zum Ausdruck bringen wollte.

8. Mißverständnisse und Unklarheiten beseitigen

I'm afraid I didn't express myself clearly. Let me put it this way: ...	Ich fürchte, ich habe mich nicht deutlich ausgedrückt. Lassen Sie es mich so sagen: ...
Sorry. I'm probably not making my-self clear. Let me put it another way.	Tut mir leid. Ich habe mich vielleicht nicht klar ausgedrückt. Lassen Sie es mich anders sagen.
Perhaps I should make this clearer by saying ...	Vielleicht sollte ich es verdeut-lichen, in dem ich es so formu-liere ...
Perhaps I haven't made myself clear. What I'm trying to say is this: ...	Ich habe mich vielleicht unklar aus-gedrückt. Was ich versuche, Ihnen zu sagen, ist folgendes: ...
Perhaps if I might explain in more detail it would clarify the misunder-standing.	Wenn ich vielleicht tiefer in die Einzelheiten gehen dürfte, würde es das Mißverständnis klären.
Allow me to rephrase that ...	Lassen Sie es mich anders formulieren ...
In other words ...	Mit anderen Worten ...
To be more specific ...	Um es genauer zu sagen ...
In simpler terms ...	Einfacher ausgedrückt ...
Let's put our cards on the table.	Legen wir die Karten auf den Tisch.

Beeinflussen, Überreden, Überzeugen

1. Wie man Bedenken zerstreut

There's no need to worry.	Es besteht kein Anlaß zur Besorgnis.
There's no cause for concern.	Es gibt keinen Grund zur Besorgnis.
There's no reason to be alarmed.	Es gibt keinen Grund zur Beunruhigung.
I can assure you that ...	Ich kann Ihnen versichern, daß ...
Let me reassure you on that point.	Was das anbetrifft, so kann ich Sie beruhigen.
I share your concern about ... and I assure you that ...	Ich teile Ihre Besorgnis über ... und versichere Ihnen, daß ...
I understand your apprehensions. But they are unfounded.	Ich verstehe Ihre Befürchtungen. Aber sie sind unbegründet.
Let me assure you, you need have no fears about ...	Ich darf Ihnen versichern, daß Sie keine Angst wegen ... zu haben brauchen.
We will do everything in our power to ...	Wir werden alles in unserer Macht Stehende tun, um zu ...
Your apprehensions are unfounded.	Ihre Befürchtungen sind unbegründet.

2. Eigene Argumente in die Diskussion einbringen

I wonder if you've taken into account the fact that ...	Ich frage mich, ob Sie berücksichtigt haben, daß ...
So far you've only mentioned the arguments in favour of ... . However, we should bear in mind that ...	Bis jetzt haben Sie nur die Argumente dafür erwähnt. Wir sollten jedoch nicht vergessen, daß ...
I think there's more to say about this project. Have you thought of ... ?	Ich glaube, über dieses Projekt ist noch mehr zu sagen. Haben Sie an ... gedacht?

I wonder if you've considered ....?	Ich frage mich, ob Sie ... berücksichtigt haben?
Seen from another angle, one could say ...	Unter einem anderen Blickwinkel betrachtet, könnte man sagen ...
If we look at it in another light, the figures look less favourable.	Bei anderem Licht betrachtet, sehen die Zahlen nicht so günstig aus.
There are other considerations. For example ...	Es gibt noch andere Überlegungen. Zum Beispiel ...
There are, if I might say so, certain points you shouldn't ignore.	Es gibt gewisse Punkte, die Sie, wenn ich das sagen darf, nicht außer acht lassen sollten.

3. Suggestiv- und Scheinfragen

Wouldn't you agree that ...?	Würden Sie mir nicht zustimmen, daß ... ?
Wouldn't it be a good idea to ...?	Wäre es nicht eine gute Idee, zu ...?
Do you realise that ...?	Ist Ihnen bewußt, daß ...?
Has it occurred to you that ...?	Haben Sie daran gedacht, daß ...?
Have you taken into account ...?	Haben Sie berücksichtigt, daß ...?
I've been wondering for the last thirty minutes if you've thought of ...?	Ich habe mich die letzte halbe Stunde gefragt, ob Sie an ... gedacht haben?

4. Den Redner vorsichtig angreifen oder herausfordern

Your enthusiasm is contagious.But when are you going to give us some hard facts?	Ihre Begeisterung ist ansteckend. Aber wann liefern Sie uns harte Fakten?
Your presentation has been most entertaining. Are there any facts to follow?	Ihre Präsentation war sehr unterhaltsam. Können wir noch mit einigen Tatsachen rechnen?
I think we shouldn't jump to conclusions.	Ich meine, wir sollten keine voreiligen Schlüsse ziehen.

Are you really trying to make us believe that ...?	Wollen Sie uns wirklich glauben machen, daß ...?
I would be inclined to be more careful, if I were you.	An Ihrer Stelle wäre ich wohl etwas vorsichtiger.
I don't think you fully appreciate the fact that ...	Ich glaube nicht, daß Sie die Tatsache voll berücksichtigen, daß ...
I wonder if that view is justified in the light of costing.	Ich frage mich, ob diese Meinung angesichts der Kosten gerechtfertigt ist.

5. Eine Entscheidung oder Abstimmung blockieren

I've certain reservations about/as to ...	Ich habe einige Vorbehalte bezüglich/hinsichtlich ...
I can't help feeling that we need some more information on that.	Ich habe einfach das Gefühl, daß wir noch mehr Informationen darüber benötigen.
I think we should give ourselves time to think everything over.	Ich meine, wir sollten uns mehr Zeit gönnen, um alles noch einmal zu überdenken.
I'm afraid a decision at this stage might lead to ...	Ich fürchte, eine Entscheidung zu diesem Zeitpunkt könnte dazu führen, daß ...
Under no circumstances should we come to a hasty decision.	Wir sollten auf keinen Fall eine voreilige Entscheidung treffen.
I think we shouldn't be rushed into making a premature decision.	Ich denke, wir sollten uns nicht zu einer verfrühten Entscheidung drängen lassen.
I feel that it would be wiser to postpone a vote until all the facts are available.	Ich bin der Meinung, daß es klüger wäre, eine Abstimmung zu verschieben, bis alle Fakten auf dem Tisch sind.

Vorschläge machen

1. Vorschläge in neutralem Ton

I propose that ...	Ich schlage vor, daß ...
I suggest that ...	Ich schlage vor/rege an, daß ...
I advise you ...	Ich rate Ihnen ...
I recommend that ...	Ich empfehle, daß ...
My proposal is ...	Mein Vorschlag ist ...
My suggestion is ...	Mein Vorschlag ist ...
My recommendation is ...	Meine Empfehlung lautet ...
My advice is ...	Mein Rat ist ...

2. Vorschläge vorsichtig einbringen

Might it be an idea if we ...?	Wäre es nicht gut, wenn wir ...?
Wouldn't it be better to/if ...?	Wäre es nicht besser, zu/ wenn ...?
Don't you think it might be a good idea to ...?	Meinen Sie nicht, daß es eine gute Idee wäre, zu ...?
What about buying this patent?	Wie wäre es, wenn wir das Patent kauften?
How about postponing the decision?	Wie wäre es, wenn wir die Entscheidung aufschieben würden?
Why don't we put it to the vote?	Warum stimmen wir nicht darüber ab?
Why not take an early flight?	Warum nehmen wir nicht einfach einen frühen Flug?
Wouldn't it be wiser to wait?	Wäre es nicht klüger zu warten?
I would propose that we accept the offer.	Ich würde vorschlagen, daß wir das Angebot annehmen.
I would recommend rejecting the offer.	Ich würde empfehlen, das Angebot abzulehnen.

I would suggest that we put off the decision.	Ich würde vorschlagen, daß wir die Entscheidung aufschieben.
I wonder if I might suggest something? Hadn't we better wait until we have some more information?	Dürfte ich etwas vorschlagen? Wäre es nicht ratsamer zu warten, bis wir mehr Informationen haben?
I would like to put forward a proposal. We could ...	Ich würde gerne einen Vorschlag machen. Wir könnten ...
May I submit a proposal?	Darf ich einen Vorschlag unterbreiten?
If I may/might make a suggestion, we could ...	Wenn ich einen Vorschlag machen darf/dürfte? Wir könnten ...
We might just as well try to ...	Wir könnten genausogut versuchen, zu ...

3. Vorschläge mit Nachdruck versehen

In my eyes it's high time we did something. I suggest that ...	In meinen Augen ist es höchste Zeit, daß wir etwas unternehmen. Ich schlage vor, daß ...
I strongly recommend that ...	Ich empfehle dringend, daß ...
I advise you most strongly to adopt this motion.	Ich rate Ihnen dringend, diesen Antrag anzunehmen.
I'm convinced that my proposal is the only feasible one.	Ich bin überzeugt, daß mein Vorschlag der einzig machbare ist.
I think the only realistic alternative is ...	Ich denke, die einzige realistische Alternative ist ...
In our view, the most promising solution is the following: ...	In unseren Augen ist die vielversprechendste Lösung folgende: ...

4. Zu Vorschlägen Stellung nehmen

Perhaps you've got a point there. Let's go through your suggestions one by one.	Sie haben damit vielleicht recht. Gehen wir Ihre Vorschläge Punkt für Punkt durch.
I can go along with your proposal.	Ich kann mich Ihrem Vorschlag anschließen.

I have some sympathy with your proposal, but please remember ...	Ich kann mich mit Ihrem Vorschlag anfreunden, aber bitte bedenken Sie ...
You've convinced me.	Sie haben mich überzeugt.
Are you really suggesting we should buy from this retailer?	Schlagen Sie wirklich vor, daß wir von diesem Einzelhändler kaufen sollen?
That's all very well, but ...	Das ist alles schön und gut, aber ...
Your suggestion is easier said than done.	Dein Vorschlag ist leichter gesagt als getan.

Zustimmung und Ablehnung ausdrücken

1. Teilweise einverstanden sein

Well, I agree in principle, but ...	Ich bin prinzipiell einverstanden, aber ...
I agree in general with you, however, it could be said that ...	Ich stimme Ihnen im allgemeinen zu, jedoch könnte man anmerken, daß ...
I agree with you on this point, but ...	In diesem Punkt bin ich einverstanden, aber ...
You may be partly right. Even so ...	Sie mögen teilweise recht haben. Trotzdem ....
I see your point, but please remember that ...	Ich verstehe, was Sie meinen, aber denken Sie bitte daran, daß ...
I agree up to a point, but ...	Bis zu einem gewissen Punkt teile ich Ihre Meinung, aber ...
To a certain extent I agree with you, but ...	Bis zu einem gewissen Punkt teile ich Ihre Meinung, aber ...
I agree with you about the practicability of ... . However ...	Was die Machbarkeit von ... angeht, stimme ich Ihnen zu. Jedoch...
I have some sympathy with your position, but please remember ...	Ich verstehe Ihren Standpunkt, aber bitte bedenken Sie ...
Well, I don't disagree altogether, but are you aware of the fact that ...	Nun gut, wir sind uns nicht völlig uneins, aber ist Ihnen bewußt, daß ...

I can see your point of view, but have you considered ...	Ich verstehe Ihren Standpunkt, aber haben Sie auch bedacht ...
I agree up to a point but I'm not totally convinced.	Ich stimme mit Ihnen bis zu einem gewissen Grad überein, bin aber nicht völlig überzeugt.
You have a certain point there, but I'm afraid it's not as easy as you think.	Sie haben nicht ganz unrecht, aber ich fürchte es ist nicht so leicht, wie Sie denken.
I can go along with you up to a certain point, however ...	Ich kann mich Ihnen teilweise anschließen, jedoch ...
In theory your are right, but how will it work in practice?	Theoretisch haben Sie recht, aber wird das in der Praxis klappen?

2. Einverständnis ausdrücken

I agree.	Ich bin einverstanden/bin Ihrer Meinung
I can see your point.	Ich verstehe, was Sie meinen.
I think you are right.	Ich glaube, Sie haben recht.
I think we've come to an agreement.	Ich glaube, wir sind uns jetzt einig.
I can go along with your proposal.	Ich kann mich Ihrem Vorschlag anschließen.
I can go along with your suggestion.	Ich kann mich Ihrem Vorschlag anschließen.
I share your view that ...	Ich teile Ihre Ansicht, daß ...
You have a point there.	Darin/damit haben Sie recht.
I think we are in agreement on that.	Ich denke, wir sind darüber einer Meinung.
I think we can accept your position on that.	Ich glaube, wir können Ihren Standpunkt in dieser Sache akzeptieren.
I'd like to support this proposal.	Ich würde diesen Vorschlag gerne unterstützen.

3. Volle Übereinstimmung betonen

I completely agree.	Ich pflichte Ihnen voll und ganz bei.
I totally agree with you.	Ich bin mit Ihnen völlig einer Meinung.
I agree entirely with your point of view.	Ich sehe die Dinge genauso wie Sie.
I'm exactly of the same opinion.	Ich bin genau der gleichen Meinung.
We're in total agreement.	Wir sind uns völlig einig.
We see eye to eye in this affair.	Wir verstehen uns, was diese Angelegenheit betrifft.
I couldn't agree more.	Ich bin völlig Ihrer Meinung.
Here's to our contract.	Stoßen wir auf unseren Vertrag an.

4. Redewendungen, die Ablehnung einleiten

I'm afraid ...	Ich fürchte, .../ Leider ...
Actually, ...	Eigentlich ...
In fact, ...	Tatsächlich .../Eigentlich ...
As a matter of fact ...	Eigentlich .../Ehrlich gesagt, ...
Frankly, ...	Ehrlich gesagt, ...
To be honest, ...	Um ehrlich zu sein, ...
In those circumstances ...	Unter diesen Umständen ...
Don't take it wrong, but ...	Nehmen Sie es nicht übel, aber ...
Excuse me, but ...	Entschuldigen Sie, aber ...

5. Freundliche Ablehnung

I see what you mean, although ...	Ich verstehe, was sie meinen, obwohl ...
You seem to have a point there. All the same ...	Sie scheinen da nicht ganz unrecht zu haben. Trotzdem ...
I'd like to agree. Nevertheless ...	Ich würde Ihnen gerne zustimmen. Dennoch ...

Do you really think so? I have my doubts.	Glauben Sie wirklich? Ich habe da meine Zweifel.
I see it a little differently.	Ich sehe das etwas anders.
I have some sympathy with your position, but please remember ...	Ihr Standpunkt ist mir nicht ganz fremd, aber bitte bedenken Sie ...
You have a point there, but I'm afraid it's not as easy as you think.	Sie haben nicht ganz unrecht, aber ich fürchte, es ist nicht so leicht, wie Sie denken.
I still have my doubts.	Ich habe immer noch Zweifel.

6. Neutrale Ablehnung

I can't quite agree with you, Bryan.	Ich kann dir da nicht ganz zustimmen, Bryan.
You're entitled to your point of view. But allow me to see it a little differently.	Sie haben ein Recht auf Ihre Meinung. Aber gestatten Sie mir, daß ich dies etwas anders sehe.
With respect, I see it a little differently.	Nehmen Sie es mir nicht übel, aber ich sehe dies ein bißchen anders.
I'm afraid I can't quite agree with you.	Ich kann Ihnen leider nicht ganz zustimmen.
I'm afraid we are in disagreement.	Ich fürchte, wir sind verschiedener Ansicht.
I'm afraid I can't say that I share your view.	Ich kann leider nicht sagen, daß ich Ihre Meinung teile.
I'm sorry, I can't go along with you.	Tut mir leid, aber ich kann Ihre Meinung nicht teilen.
I'm not totally convinced by your argument.	Ihr Argument hat mich nicht völlig überzeugt.
I can't help feeling that I must disagree.	Ich kann leider nicht anders, ich bin anderer Meinung.
I really can't share your opinion about this project.	Ich kann Ihre Meinung zu dem Projekt wirklich nicht teilen.

I simply can't accept your conclusion.	Ich kann Ihre Schlußfolgerung einfach nicht akzeptieren.
I'm afraid I can't see your point there.	Tut mir leid, aber ich verstehe nicht, was Sie meinen.
I can't accept your position on that.	Ich kann Ihren Standpunkt dazu nicht akzeptieren.
Let's stop splitting hairs.	Hören wir auf, Haare zu spalten.
We'll have to agree to differ.	Wir sind uns einig, daß wir verschiedener Meinung sind.

7. Entschiedener Widerspruch

With respect, I disagree entirely.	Nehmen Sie es nicht übel, ich bin ganz anderer Meinung.
I respect your opinion, however ...	Ich respektiere Ihre Meinung, jedoch ...
With due respect, what you are saying is impossible to implement.	Ihre Meinung in Ehren, aber was Sie da sagen, läßt sich unmöglich durchführen.
I totally disagree with you on that.	Ich bin darüber völlig anderer Meinung als Sie.
I'm sorry, but I don't agree at all.	Es tut mir leid, aber ich kann auf keinen Fall zustimmen.
To be quite frank, I think you're mistaken.	Um ganz ehrlich zu sein, ich glaube, Sie irren sich.
To put it bluntly, your arguments don't hold water.	Um es ungeschminkt zu sagen, Ihre Argumente sind nicht stichhaltig.
I must take issue with you over these figures.	Was diese Zahlen anbetrifft, so muß ich Ihnen widersprechen.
I must strongly protest against ...	Ich muß entschieden gegen ... protestieren.
We are not entirely convinced that this is a viable solution.	Wir sind nicht völlig davon überzeugt, daß dies eine dauerhafte Lösung ist.

8. Enttäuschung ausdrücken	
Frankly, Mr Brain, we had hoped for more.	Ehrlich gesagt, Herr Brain, wir hätten mehr erwartet.
It's a bit disappointing that ...	Es ist etwas enttäuschend, daß ...
I'm rather disappointed with the performance of this robot.	Ich bin ziemlich enttäuscht von der Leistung dieses Roboters.
You've really let us down.	Sie haben uns wirklich im Stich gelassen.
It's a great shame that ...	Es ist eine Schande, daß ...

9. Ausrufe des Protests	
Definitely not!	Bestimmt nicht!
Come off it!	Hören Sie doch auf damit!
You must be joking!	Sie machen wohl Witze!
Nonsense!	Unsinn!
Ridiculous!	Lächerlich!
Rubbish!	Quatsch!

Wie man Kompromisse findet

1. Kompromisse vorschlagen	
We are ready to meet you halfway.	Wir sind bereit, Ihnen auf halbem Wege entgegenzukommen.
Let's strike/make a compromise.	Machen wir einen Kompromiß.
What we need is a compromise solution where both of us walk away from this table with something in our hands.	Was wir brauchen, ist eine Kompromißlösung, mit der wir beide vom Tisch aufstehen können und etwas in der Hand haben.
We are prepared to make certain concessions.	Wir sind bereit, gewisse Zugeständnisse zu machen.

I think it is still possible to strike a compromise.	Ich glaube, es ist immer noch möglich, einen Kompromiß zu finden.
Perhaps we should compromise rather than go to court.	Vielleicht sollten wir einen Kompromiß schließen, anstatt zu prozessieren.
I'm sure we can somehow come to an agreement.	Ich bin sicher, wir werden uns irgendwie einig werden.

2. Kompromisse an Bedingungen knüpfen

We would be ready to sign, provided that ...	Wir wären bereit zu unterschreiben, vorausgesetzt, daß ...
We would be willing to accept your offer, providing ...	Wir wären bereit, Ihr Angebot zu akzeptieren, vorausgesetzt, daß ...
We would be prepared to give you a reduction on condition that ...	Wir wären bereit, Ihnen einen Preisnachlaß zu gewähren, unter der Bedingung, daß ...
I think we could agree to your suggestion on condition that ...	Ich denke, wir könnten Ihrem Vorschlag zustimmen, unter der Bedingung, daß ...
We are willing to ... with the provision that ...	Wir sind bereit zu ... unter dem Vorbehalt, daß ...
We are more than ready to buy from you as long as you are ready to ...	Wir sind durchaus geneigt, bei Ihnen zu kaufen, wenn Sie bereit sind, zu ...

3. Gegenbedingungen aufstellen

If you would be prepared to ..., then we would be ready to ...	Wenn Sie bereit wären zu ... , dann wären wir einverstanden zu ...
If you would be willing to ... then we could ...	Wenn Sie bereit wären zu ..., dann könnten wir ...
If we agree, we hope you would reciprocate by ...	Wenn wir zustimmen, dann hoffen wir, daß Sie sich mit .... revanchieren werden.
If we agree it would be conditional on ...	Wenn wir zustimmen, wäre das abhängig von ...

We see no objection, provided that ...	Wir sehen keine Einwände, unter der Voraussetzung, daß ...
Only if you ..., would we be prepared to ...	Nur wenn Sie ..., wären wir bereit zu ...
I don't think we could accept, unless you gave us a reduction of 3 per cent.	Ich glaube nicht, daß wir annehmen können, es sei denn, Sie gewähren uns einen Nachlaß von 3 Prozent.
We'd be rather reluctant to accept, unless you guarantee that ...	Wir könnten nur sehr schwer zustimmen, es sei denn, Sie garantieren, daß ...

4. Fragen, ob ein Kompromiß annehmbar ist

Is that acceptable?	Ist das annehmbar?
Would that be satisfactory?	Wäre das zufriedenstellend?
Would that be a basis for a compromise?	Wäre das eine Basis für einen Kompromiß?
Would that be acceptable as a compromise solution.	Wäre dies eine annehmbare Kompromißlösung?
We hope that this will be negotiable.	Wir hoffen, daß dies verhandlungsfähig ist.

5. Einem Kompromiß zustimmen

We have no objection to that.	Wir haben keinen Einwand dagegen.
I think that would be acceptable.	Ich glaube, das wäre annehmbar.
That seems to be a reasonable compromise.	Dies scheint ein vernünftiger Kompromiß zu sein.
I think we could agree to your condition.	Ich glaube, wir können Ihrer Bedingung zustimmen.
Let's hope we don't live to regret it.	Wollen wir hoffen, daß wir es nicht zu bereuen haben.

6. Wie man Kompromißvorschläge ablehnt

You put us in a difficult position.	Sie bringen uns in eine schwierige Lage.
I'm afraid we are obliged to reject the proposal.	Ich fürchte, wir müssen diesen Vorschlag ablehnen.
You leave us with little alternative but to reject the compromise.	Sie lassen uns keinen anderen Ausweg, als diesen Kompromiß abzulehnen.
In that case, we should very reluctantly have to reject the compromise.	In diesem Fall müßten wir den Kompromiß schweren Herzens ablehnen.
Although we want to avoid a deadlock as much as you do, we find your suggestion unacceptable.	Obwohl wir eine Pattsituation genausosehr vermeiden wollen wie Sie, halten wir Ihren Vorschlag für unanehmbar.
We are not entirely convinced that this is a viable solution.	Wir sind nicht völlig davon überzeugt, daß dies eine dauerhafte Lösung ist.
You're driving a hard bargain. We cannot but reject the compromise.	Sie sind ein harter Verhandlungspartner. Wir können nicht anders, als den Kompromiß abzulehnen.

Sprache und Strategie der Präsentation

1. Stellen Sie sich vor – betonen Sie Gemeinsamkeiten

I'm Otto Daimler.	Ich bin Otto Daimler.
I spent three years in Britain which is, by the way, where I had this little idea of ...	Ich habe drei Jahre in England verbracht, dort ist mir übrigens die Idee gekommen zu ...
I have been a consultant to ICS for three years.	Ich war drei Jahre als Berater bei ICS tätig.

I know your problems since I was salesmanager like most of you.	Ich kenne Ihre Probleme, da ich wie die meisten von Ihnen Verkaufsmanager gewesen bin.
I'm no more expert in this field than you are.	Ich bin auf diesem Gebiet auch nicht mehr Fachmann als Sie.

2. Bedanken Sie sich beim Publikum

I'm glad to have the chance to speak to you about ...	Ich freue mich, daß ich die Gelegenheit habe, zu Ihnen über ... zu sprechen.
I'm grateful for having been offered the opportunity to present our product range.	Ich bin dankbar, daß man mir Gelegenheit gibt, Ihnen unsere Produktpalette vorzustellen.
I appreciate that you're sacrificing one hour of your valuable time to listen to me.	Ich bin Ihnen dankbar, daß Sie eine Stunde Ihrer wertvollen Zeit opfern, um mir zuzuhören.
Ladies and gentlemen, I'd like to thank you for your time.	Meine Damen und Herren, ich möchte mich für Ihre Zeit bedanken.
Don't hesitate to interrupt me when you have a question.	Zögern Sie nicht, mich zu unterbrechen, wenn Sie eine Frage haben.

3. Das Thema ankündigen

Now you've met here today to hear something about our ideas on ...	Sie sind heute hier zusammengekommen, um etwas über unsere Vorstellungen von ... zu hören.
The topic of this presentation is ...	Gegenstand dieser Präsentation ist ...
The subject of today's presentation is ...	Das Thema der heutigen Präsentation ist ...
In my presentation I'll be explaining our new project.	In meiner Präsentation werde ich unser neues Projekt erläutern.
What I'm going to explain this afternoon are the problems involved in ...	Heute nachmittag will ich Ihnen die Probleme im Zusammenhang mit ... erklären.

I'll be presenting my latest invention.	Ich werde meine neueste Erfindung vorstellen.
This morning I'd like to look back at the past fiscal year.	Heute früh will ich einen Rückblick auf das letzte Geschäftsjahr geben.
I'm trying to give you an overview of the development of our company's activities in Asia.	Ich versuche Ihnen einen Überblick zu geben, wie sich die Aktivitäten unserer Firma in Asien entwickelt haben.

4. Auf Tischvorlagen hinweisen

In the handout which I'll be passing round, you'll find ...	In den Tischvorlagen, die ich herumgehen lasse, finden Sie ...
In the folder which I'll be distributing, you'll find the copies of the OHP transparencies / foils.	In dem Ordner, den ich austeile, finden Sie die Kopien der Overheadfolien.
I've prepared a detailed cost breakdown, which I'll be handing round now.	Ich habe eine detaillierte Kostenaufstellung vorbereitet, die ich nun austeilen werde.
As you all know from your pre-conference handouts ...	Wie Sie alle Ihren Unterlagen entnommen haben, die Ihnen vor der Besprechung zugegangen sind, ...
May I draw your attention to the handout in front of you?	Darf ich Ihre Aufmerksamkeit auf die Tischvorlage vor Ihnen lenken?

5. Einen Überblick geben, Gliederung vorstellen

My presentation will be in three main parts.	Meine Präsentation gliedert sich in drei Teile.
I'll be developing the three major stages of our project.	Ich werde Ihnen die drei wichtigsten Stufen unseres Projekts schildern.
In the first part of my presentation I'll ...	Im ersten Teil meiner Präsentation werde ich ...
Then, in the second part of the meeting, there will be a period for free discussion and question time.	Im zweiten Teil unserer Besprechung folgt eine Runde für Diskussionen und Fragen.

Firstly, I'd like to ... Secondly, we could ... And I'll finish with ...	Zuerst würde ich gerne ... Zweitens könnten wir ... Und ich werde schließen mit ...
First, I'll give you an overview of ... Then I'll ... Lastly ...	Zuerst gebe ich Ihnen einen Überblick über ... Dann werde ich ... Schließlich ...

6. Orientierungshilfen geben, Schritte deutlich machen

I'll begin by summarising the problems we're having with ...	Ich beginne mit einer Zusammenfassung der Probleme, die wir mit ... haben.
To begin with, let me say ...	Lassen Sie mich einleitend sagen ...
Let's start with ...	Fangen wir mit ... an.
I'd like to begin my presentation by giving you an overview of the project.	Ich würde meiner Präsentation gerne einen Überblick über das Projekt voranstellen.
If I could now turn to ...	Wenn wir uns nun ... zuwenden können.
Let me now move on to ...	Lassen Sie mich nun zu ... kommen.
So that's the present situation. Now let's look at ...	Das ist also die gegenwärtige Situation. Betrachten wir nun ...
Let me now come to my other functions.	Lassen Sie mich nun auf die anderen Funktionen zu sprechen kommen.
That completes my overview of ...	Damit ist mein Überblick über ... abgeschlossen.

7. Problembewußtsein durch rhetorische Fragen aktivieren

What's the explanation for this?	Welche Erklärung gibt es dafür?
How can we explain this?	Wie können wir dies erklären?
What can we do about this?	Was können wir dagegen tun?
How will this affect us?	Inwieweit betrifft uns dies?
What are the implications for the company?	Was sind die Folgen für die Firma?

How can we benefit from this development?	Wie können wir von dieser Entwicklung profitieren ?
Is there a simple solution to the problem?	Gibt es eine einfache Lösung zu diesem Problem?
What are the benefits from this situation?	Welchen Nutzen ziehen wir aus dieser Situation?
Now what about the advantages?	Nun, wo liegen die Vorteile?

8. Gründe und Lösungen anbieten

There are two reasons for this. First ... Second ...	Es gibt zwei Gründe dafür. Erstens ... Zweitens ...
This is due to two factors. Firstly ... Secondly ...	Zwei Faktoren sind dafür verantwortlich. Erstens ... Zweitens ...
One reason for this is ... Another reason is ...	Ein Grund dafür ist ... Ein weiterer Grund ist ...
The main reason for this is ...	Der hauptsächliche Grund dafür ist ...
A particular reason for this is ...	Ein besonderer Grund dafür ist ...
A key problem is ...	Ein Schlüsselproblem ist ...
Therefore we have to ...	Deshalb müssen wir ...
One way to solve the problem is ...	Eine Möglichkeit, das Problem zu lösen, ist ...
Because of this ...	Deswegen ...
As a result ...	Darum ... Also ...
Consequently ...	Folglich ...

9. Die Zuhörer auf Anschauungsmaterial vorbereiten

Well, before I start can everybody see the screen?	Bevor ich beginne, können alle die Leinwand sehen?
If you can move your chairs in a little.	Wenn Sie vielleicht Ihre Stühle ein bißchen zusammenrücken würden.

I'll use the flipchart here for any spontaneous points which might arise.	Ich werde alle Punkte, die spontan auftauchen könnten, auf dieser Flipchart festhalten.
First, I'd like to show you several OHP sheets to explain the technical details.	Zuerst würde ich Ihnen gerne einige Folien zeigen, um die technischen Details zu klären.
The next slide shows ...	Das nächste Dia zeigt ...
Now I'll show you ...	Nun zeige ich Ihnen ...
Let's now look at the figures for ...	Betrachten wir nun die Zahlen für ...

10. Die Aufmerksamkeit des Publikums lenken

As you can see from this chart ...	Wie Sie dem Diagramm entnehmen können, ...
Observe the difference between ...	Beobachten Sie den Unterschied zwischen ...
Notice the movement of the robot.	Beachten Sie die Bewegungen des Roboters.
What is interesting to notice is ...	Es ist interessant zu sehen, daß ...
It is interesting to notice that ...	Es ist interessant zu sehen, daß ...
If we look more closely at X ...	Wenn wir X genauer betrachten ...
Please, look at the upper right-hand corner of the diagram.	Betrachten Sie nun die obere rechte Ecke der Grafik.
The upper part of the slide shows the interior of the container.	Der obere Teil des Dias zeigt das Innere des Behälters.
This chart compares turnover in two countries.	Dieses Diagramm vergleicht die Umsätze in den beiden Ländern.
You can see here the development over the past year.	Sie können hier die Entwicklung im letzten Jahr verfolgen.

11. Alternativen aufzeigen

Let's consider the options ...	Betrachten wir die Alternativen ...
The first option is to ...	Die erste Möglichkeit ist ...
Let's go through the possibilities ...	Gehen wir die Möglichkeiten durch ...
What alternatives have we got ... ?	Welche Alternativen haben wir ...?
On one hand we could ...	Einerseits könnten wir ...
On the other hand, one could try to ...	Andererseits könnte man versuchen zu ...
However, there is another alternative.	Jedoch gibt es noch eine weitere Alternative.
One way to solve the problem is to ...	Eine Möglichkeit, das Problem zu lösen, ist ...
But what about the second option?	Aber wie steht es mit der zweiten Alternative?
Now let's look at a third option.	Betrachten wir nun die dritte Möglichkeit.
Let's first look at the benefits.	Betrachten wir zuerst die Vorteile.
There are, however, disadvantages, too.	Es gibt jedoch auch Nachteile.

12. Zuhörerfragen wiederholen und Bedenkzeit gewinnen

I'd be happy to answer any questions.	Ich beantworte gerne jeder Ihrer Fragen.
If you've any questions, I'd be pleased to answer them now.	Wenn Sie irgendwelche Fragen haben, würde ich sie jetzt gerne beantworten.
I'd welcome any comments.	Ich würde mich über jeden Kommentar freuen.
So, what you're asking is why we ...	Sie fragen also, warum wir ...

If I understand your question correctly, you would like to know ...	Wenn ich Ihre Frage richtig verstehe, wollen Sie wissen ...
So, do we plan to increase salaries?	Also, planen wir die Gehälter zu erhöhen?
When you say ...do you mean ...?	Wenn Sie sagen ..., meinen Sie damit ...?
I'm sorry, could you please repeat your question?	Entschuldigen Sie, könnten Sie Ihre Frage bitte wiederholen?

13. Vorsichtiger Umgang mit Teilnehmerkritik

Yes, I quite see your point. However, you'll admit that ...	Ja, ich verstehe schon, was Sie meinen. Jedoch werden Sie zugeben, daß ...
Yes, it's something we've thought about a lot,too, but ...	Ja, das ist etwas, worüber wir auch viel nachgedacht haben, aber ...
That's an accurate observation. On the other hand, if we consider that ...	Das ist eine richtige Beobachtung. Andererseits, wenn wir berücksichtigen, daß ...
I know it's difficult to accept this decision, but the evidence is there.	Ich weiß, es ist schwer, diese Entscheidung zu akzeptieren, aber die Beweise liegen auf der Hand.

14. Kritik und Fragen ausweichen

I'm afraid I'm not the right person to answer that.	Ich fürchte, ich bin nicht die richtige Person, um diese Frage zu beantworten.
Dr. Hill is a much better person to answer that.	Dr. Hill kann diese Frage viel besser beantworten als ich.
I'm not sure this is the right place to discuss this particular question.	Ich weiß nicht, ob hier der richtige Ort ist, diese spezielle Frage zu diskutieren.
Could we leave that for later?	Könnten wir uns das für später aufheben?

15. Rückblick und Zusammenfassung

Now we've come full circle.	Der Kreis hat sich nun geschlossen.
So, as we've seen in this presentation today ...	Wie wir heute in dieser Präsentation gesehen haben ...
Let me run through the main arguments again.	Lassen Sie mich die Hauptargumente noch einmal zusammenfassen.
Let us go over the main points again.	Schauen wir uns noch einmal die wichtigsten Punkte an.
To put it in a nutshell ...	In einem Wort ...
So to summarise we can say that ...	Zusammenfassend können wir also sagen, daß ...

16. Wie man sich verabschiedet

If you should have any further questions feel free to phone me up.	Sollten Sie noch irgendwelche Fragen haben, können Sie mich ruhig anrufen.
Thank you for your attention, ladies and gentlemen	Vielen Dank für Ihre Aufmerksamkeit, meine Damen und Herren.
So that was it for today. Thank you for your attention.	So, das war's für heute. Vielen Dank für Ihre Aufmerksamkeit
Thank you for being here. I hope you enjoyed it.	Danke, daß Sie gekommen sind. Ich hoffe, es hat Ihnen gefallen.

Key to the exercises

Chapter 1

Task 2: Brain test
1b, 2a, 3c

Task 3: Match work

1)	Perhaps I could return to your question later on.	**c**	refusal to be interrupted
2)	Coming back to what I was trying to explain ...	**b**	resuming
3)	Excuse me, could I just break in a moment here?	**a**	interrupting

Task 4: Patch work
Could I just *interrupt* you a moment?
If we *might* just *finish* our conversation.
Please let me finish my *sentence.*
As I was *saying,* shall we go for it?
To return to my *subject* ...
Perhaps I could *return* to your question later on ...
Coming back to what I was trying to explain ...
Excuse me, could I just *break in* a moment here?

Task 5: Form and function
"If I may just interrupt you a moment," is the most formal.
"Hold on" is the least formal function.

Task 6: Mind your manners

Can I just break in a moment here?	Could I just break in a moment here?
If I may just say a few words about ...	If I might just say a few words about ...
If I could just come in here.	If I may just come in here.
If I may just go back to the point I was making.	If I might just go back to the point I was making.

Chapter 2

Task 2: Brain test

1b, 2b, 3a

Task 3: Match work

1)	As you can see from the agenda ...	**b**	announcing the purpose
2)	Right, shall we get started?	**a**	opening a meeting
3)	I'd like to call it a day now.	**d**	closing a meeting
4)	That's not the right attitude.	**c**	keeping up discipline

Task 4: Patch work

I *declare* the meeting open.
Has everyone received a copy of the *agenda*?
Bryan has volunteered to keep the *minutes*.
The *objective / purpose* of this meeting is to establish a new company.
The *purpose / objective* of today's meeting is ...
Now to the reason for my *calling* this meeting.
Let's get down to business, *shall we*?
Is there anything else to *discuss*?
I'd like to *draw* this meeting to a close.
I declare the meeting *closed*. Thank you, Ladies and Gentlemen.

Task 5: Form and function

Look, Amy, couldn't we discuss that later and take item one now?

Task 6: Mind your manners

That is impossible.	Is that possible ?
That is unacceptable.	Is that acceptable?
Is that possible?	Would that be possible?
I'm afraid that is impossible.	I'm afraid that would be impossible.
I couldn't agree.	I wouldn't be able to agree.

Chapter 3

Task 2: Brain test

1a) The text does not say why.

2a) The original idea of ICS Ltd.

3b,c) They will collect the missing information about potential markets, cost structure, promotion etc. Then they will send a written report to the bank.

Task 3: Match Work (1)

1) Let me start with ... Then I'll ...	**c**	explaining the structure
2) The objective of this presentation is to ...	**a**	announcing the purpose
3) There are three aspects I'd like to focus upon.	**b**	giving an overview

Task 4: Patch work

The *subject* of our meeting today is to ...
In my presentation I'll be *explaining* our new project.
I'll begin my presentation by giving you an *overview* of the project.
This morning I'd like to *look back* at the past fiscal year.
I'm trying to give you a *summary* of our company's activities.
I'll be developing the three *major / main parts* of our project.
To *begin with*, I'd like to show you what our robot can do
My presentation will be in *three main / major parts*.
There are three aspects I'd like to *focus upon / on*.
If I might *suggest* something. Wouldn't it be better if we took a break?

Task 5 : Match Work (2)

1) I'll be developing the three major our project.	**e**	announcing end
2) To begin with, let me say ...	**c**	introducing second part
3) Let's now turn to the problem of ...	**d**	looking at alternatives
4) Let's consider the options.	**b**	introducing first part
5) I'd like to conclude by stating ... parts of our project.	**a**	giving an overview

Task 6 : Emphasis

What I'm going to explain today is our *new project*.
What I'm trying to do is give you a summary of our *firm's activities*.
What I'll begin with is to give you an *overview* of the project.
It's a flipchart we need,Mrs Fünkner.
It's an agency (that) we will have to consult.
It's a full report on the project (that/which) they want.

Task 7: Word power

I'll be developing the three major of our project.	My presentation will be in parts three main parts.
To begin with, let me say ...	Let me start with ...
Let's now turn to the problem of ...	The next question I would like to focus on is ...
Let's consider the options	Let's go through the possibilities
I'd like to conclude by stating ...	In conclusion, I'd like to say ...

Chapter 4

Task 2: Brain test
1b, 2b, 3a

Task 3: Match work

1)	Excuse me, may I ask a question?	**c**	someone interrupts you
2)	Thank you for your question which leads us back to our main problem.	**d**	come back to your point
3)	Where do you stand on this issue?	**a**	find out what they think
4)	I think it would be fair to say ...	**b**	you say what you think

Task 4: Patch work

I'd like to hear your *views / position / opinion* on that.
What's your *position* on consulting an advertising agency?
Where exactly do you *stand* on this issue?
If you ask my *opinion* I 'm afraid an agency would be expensive.

I *tend to* think that we should consult an agency.
It *seems* to me that we should start an advertising campaign.
That *leads* us back to our main problem.
If we could come back to the *point*.
If I could *turn to* another subject.
If we could return to the *point / issue*.

Task 5: Form and function
I'm quite sure that the product will be a flop.

Task 6: Mind your manners

I'll call you back later.	Can I call you back later?
Can I ask you a question?	Could (may) I ask you a question?
That's a negative attitude.	That's not a very positve attitude
Excuse me, but I think these figures are wrong.	I beg your pardon, but aren't these figures wrong?

Task 7: What went wrong?
1) No agenda. Obviously the team don't know why they have come together.
2) No minutes. Ronald gets offensive instead of referring to the minutes.

Chapter 5

Task 2: Brain test
1c, **2**a, **3**a
4: The police put a note on his car that the road was to be repaired the following day. He didn't move the car so they towed it away.

Task 3: Match work

1) Mr Otto is going to give us a presentation of his latest invention.	**b** announcing the theme
2) That concludes our business for today. Thank you.	**e** closing the meeting

3) If we look more closely at the P.P.P., we'll notice its magic eye.	**d** focusing attention
4) I shall have to call you to order, Mr Brain.	**c** keeping the discipline
5) Right, shall we get started?	**a** opening a meeting

Task 4: Patch work

I'm glad to have the chance to *present* you my P.P.P.
I'll be *proposing* a solution to your parking problems.
To begin with / First let me give you an overview of the P.P.P.
First / To begin with I'd like to show you what my P.P.P. can do for you.
Second, I'll be *explaining* how my P.P.P. works.
I'd be *happy* to answer any of your questions.
May I *draw* your attention to the the second slide?
The *upper part* of the slide shows the P.P.P. in action.
In the *handout* that I'll be passing round you'll find the details.
Ladies and gentlemen, thank you for your *attention*.

Task 5: Mind your manners

We need more money for project.	I'm afraid we need / might need a little / bit more money for the project.
We have a cash-flow problem.	I'm afraid we have a slight cash-flow problem.
I have reservations as to the success of the P.P.P.	I have some reservations as to the success of the P.P.P.
I think that is dangerous.	I'm afraid, that is / might be a bit /little dangerous.
Send us a description of your invention.	Please send us / Could you please send us a short description of your invention.

These are only suggestions. More than one solution is possible.

Chapter 6

Task 2: Brain test

1b, 2a, 2a und **b**

Task 3: Match work

1)	Could you stick to the subject, please?	**d**	keeping discipline
2)	I'd like to support this idea of ...	**a**	agreement
3)	As well as X , there is also Y	**c**	adding new facts
4)	Let's forget formalities.	**e**	creating atmosphere
5)	How are you feeling about it, Ron?	**f**	asking for opinion
6)	I'd like to agree. Nevertheless ...	**b**	disagreement

Task 4: Patch work

Well, let's *put* it to the vote.
Those in favour *raise* their hands.
What I would like to *stress* is the usefulness of the device.
I *disagree with* you about the practicalness of the invention.
I'd like to *support* this idea of taking care of one's health.
Could you *stick to* the subject, please?
Could you keep to the *point*, Bryan?
I really can't share your *opinion* about this project.
I can *go along* with your suggestion.
I can't *quite agree* with you, Bryan.

Task 5: Form and function

I'm afraid I can't see your point there.

Task 6: Word power

1)	I see what you mean, although ...	**b**	I don't disagree altogether. Still ...
2)	With due respect, what you are saying is impossible.	**c**	To be quite frank, you're completely mistaken.
3)	I'm afraid I can't see your point there.	**a**	We'll have to agree to differ.

Chapter 7

Task 2: Brain test
1b, 2b, 3b

Task 3: Form and function
I'm most awfully sorry.

Task 4: Match work

1) Half-circle; no table	**d**	Listening to the company guru or doing autogenous training.
2) Classroom style	**e**	Briefing of larger audiences using OHP or video.
3) Conference table	**a**	Problem solving and decision taking. Use of visual aids limited.
4) Round table	**c**	A brainstorm among the engineers of the R&D Department.
5) Horseshoe	**b**	Good for larger numbers. Good for demonstrations of real objects.

Task 5: Memory work
1) Conference table **2)**Horseshoe

Task 6: Emphasise

Miss Fünkner, please *bring* in a flip-chart.	Mrs Fünkner, please *do bring* in a flip-chart.
We *expected* more information.	We *did expect* more information.
We're suggesting *cuts in production.*	*What we're suggesting* are cuts in production.
I *see* a need for change.	*I do see* a need for change
They propose a *major reorganisation.*	*What they propose* is a major reorganisation.
I *regret* that I was unable to be here earlier.	*I do* regret that I was unable to be here earlier.
More investment is needed, not cuts in investment.	*It's more investment* that is needed, not cuts in investment.

Task 7: Patch work

I do *beg* your pardon.

Never *mind*! I'm to blame, too.

I do *apologise*, young lady!

Please don't *worry*. These things happen.

I am *ever* so sorry.

It doesn't *matter*. Things like these tend to happen.

I'm most *awfully sorry*. It won't happen again.

That's *all right*. We all make mistakes, don't we?

I do *regret* that I was unable to be here earlier.

I quite *understand*. Don't worry about it.

Task 8: Match work

1)	I certainly can't see anything.	**b**	wrong room layout
2)	Here is a diagram of the model. And look at the model in front of you.	**a**	splitting attention instead of focusing it
3)	For my demonstration I need a tap. Have you an OHP?	**c**	no preparation

Chapter 8

Task 2: Form and function

Tick off the the politest or weakest form of interruption:

Excuse me, sir, may I ask a question? / I wonder if I might comment upon your last argument?

Tick off the the strongest form of reaction to an interruption:

I don't like being interrupted like this.

Task 3: Match work

1)	Well, I think we've covered everything.	**d**	announcing the end of the meeting
2)	The motion is carried by seven votes to four.	**c**	announcing the result

3)	Those in favour say 'Aye'.	**b**	counting the votes
4)	Could we move to a vote on this?	**a**	asking for a vote

Task 4: Patch work

Well, what's your *comment* on that Jikon's performance?
We wanted to ask you all for your *opinions* concerning ...
May I ask for *reactions* to Mr Jikon's presentation?
In my eyes the whole thing was a joke.
As far as I'm concerned I think it was really a giggle.
I'd say that the matter was not perfectly organised.
May I come in at this point with a practical matter?
Look here, Bryan, I don't like being *interrupted* like this.
Going back to what I was saying ... may I ask for reactions to Mr Jikon's presentation?
I suggest we *put it* to the vote.

Task 5: Mind your manners

I hoped for more.	I was hoping for more.
We should go on with the presentation.	I was wondering whether we should go on with the presentation.
We intende to make new arrangements for next year.	We were intending to make new arrangements for next year.
Have you come to a decision.	I was wondering if you'd come to a decision yet.
We discussed that yesterday, didn't we.	We were discussing that yesterday, weren't we?

Chapter 9

Task 2: Brain test

1a und **c**, **2c**, **3b**, **4a** und **c**

Task 3: Form and function

If I may make a suggestion, we could send it to Dr. Nikon.

Task 4: Complete the joke

We recommend that you pay or you'll never see him again.
Well, *may I suggest* a compromise?

Task 5: Match Work

1)	I strongly recommend that ...	**c**	I advise you most strongly to ...
2)	Why don't we ... ?	**a**	What about ...?
3)	I wonder if I might suggest ...	**d**	If I might make a suggestion.
4)	I propose that ...	**b**	I recommend that ...

Task 6: Patch work

I suggest that *we apply* for the patent immediately.
I suggest *asking* for more information first.
Why not *take* a look at other inventions?
Why don't we *send* this invention to Professor Jikon?
Wouldn't it be a good idea if you *read* the handout first?
Wouldn't it be a good idea *to ask* for an interview?
How about *applying* for a bank loan?
I recommend that we *should reject* this invention.
I recommend *putting* more flowers in the office.
Wouldn't it be better *to wait* until Ronald gets back?

Chapter 10

Task 2: Brain test

1c, 2b und **c, 3a**

Task 3: Form and function

It's A: It depends on what you mean by IMM.
The other two persons ask the speaker to confirm their own interpretations of his words.

Task 4: Match work

1) If I've understood you correctly, you're saying that ... ?	**b**	asking for confirmation
2) I'm afraid we weren't quite able to catch what you were saying.	**a**	asking for repetition
3) We seem to be talking at cross purposes.	**d**	signalling misunderstanding
4) Let me put it this way ... In simpler terms ...	**c**	clearing up misunderstandings

Task 5: Mind your manners

I'm probably not making myself clear. Let me put it another way ...

Task 6 : Patch work

Let me *put* it this way.
Could you be a little more *precise.*
With respect, that is not what I said.
We seem to be talking at cross *purposes.*
Your IMM speaks 72 languages, *doesn't he*?
You are not going to buy that robot, *are you*?
I'm afraid I'm not quite clear what you *mean* by that.
I'm afraid there seems to have been a *slight* misunderstanding.
I'm afraid we weren't quite able to *catch* what you were saying.
If I've understood you *correctly*, you're saying that IMM is a robot.

Chapter 11

Task 2: Brain test

1) IMM videotapes meetings.	T /
2) He /she prepares the agenda.	/ F
3) IMM also takes the minutes of a meeting.	T /
4) IMM corrects wrong grammar and vocabulary.	T /
5) IMM keeps up the discipline of a meeting.	T /

Task 3: Match work

1)	Mr Brain, will now speak to you.	**c**	announcing a guest speaker
2)	Mr Brain, over to you.	**d**	making someone take the floor
3)	I shall have to call you to order.	**a**	keeping discipline
4)	If I may just go over the main points.	**b**	summarising a presentation

Task 4: Patch work

First of all I will give you an overview of my main parts.
Starting at the top of the diagram you see my head.
May I *draw* your attention to the OHP sheet?
I'm afraid your statement was of little *value* here.
Your comments *add* nothing to the business of today.
I shall have to *call* you to order, young lady.
I *appreciate* that you are sacrificing one hour of your valuable time.
Don't *hesitate* to interrupt IMM when you have a question.
Mr Yudeedit, the *floor* is yours.
We're all looking *forward* to your presentation.

Task 5: Guided translation

In my presentation today I'm going to explain our *new project*.
I'll begin my presentation by giving you an *overview* of the project.
I'm trying to give you a *summary* of IMM's functions.
The *subject* of my presentation is our International Meet Master.
In my presentation I'm going to *explain* how to handle the robot.
My presentation will be in three *main parts*.

Chapter 12

Task 2: Word power

1) I'm grateful to have the chance to speak to you.	**b** I'm glad to have been offered the opportunity to present ...
2) What I'm going to explain this afternoon are the problems involved in ...	**e** What I'll be proposing in my presentation is my latest invention.
3) I'll be developing the three major parts of our project.	**d** My presentation will be in three main parts.
4) Let's consider the options.	**c** Let's go through the possibilities.
5) How will this affect us?	**a** What are the implications for the company?

Task 3: Patch work

I'm *grateful* to have the chance to speak to you.
I'll be *developing* the three major parts of our project.
Let's *consider* the options.
What are the *implications* for the company?
I'm glad to have been offered the *opportunity* to present IMM.
Let's go through the *possibilities.*
My presentation will be in three *main parts.*
What I'll be *proposing* in my presentation is my latest invention.
The *issue* under discussion is the Intelligent Meet Master.
Thank you very much for *sacrificing* some of your valuable time.

Task 5: Guided translation

I reckon / assume / suppose this robot has got a lot of potential.
I've arranged a meeting with a *potential customer prospect.*
Thank you for your *support.*
So I'll begin if there are no *further questions.*
Perhaps we could now begin with *question time.*
Mr Hemmung, let's not *get sidetracked.*

Chapter 13

Task 2: Brain test

1) What is the contract about that Ronald has signed with K&F?
They will test IMM and buy him if he behaves well.

2) Why does Nob object to this contract?
He suspects that Yudeedit has found something wrong in IMM.

3) What does Ron criticise about Bryan's body language.
He was standing in the 'pastor position'.

Task 3: Mind your manners

1	Wouldn't it be wiser to wait till we know what Yudeedit means by 'IMM could be strong, if ...'?
2	Aren't we taking too many risks, if we unleash IMM on an unsuspecting audience?
3	I'm afraid it's not as easy as that, Ron.
4	It's easier said than done to remember all those things at the same time.
5	I'm not entirely convinced that this is a good idea.
6	What you all don't seem to realise is how difficult it is to present a product.
7	I can't accept your comment that my position was all wrong.
8	Frankly, I think that is impossible.
9	I'm afraid all these comments are half-baked.

Task 4: Patch work – How to object

Frankly, I think that is *impossible.*
I'm afraid it's not *as easy as* that, Ron.
Isn't it a *bit risky* to trust this company?
I'm afraid all these comments are *half-baked.*
Are you really *convinced* that IMM will behave?
I'm not entirely convinced that this is a *good idea.*
It's *easier said* than done to remember all those things.
I can't *accept* your comment that my position was all wrong.
Wouldn't it be *wiser* to wait till Yudeedit explains what he means?
Aren't we *taking* too many risks if we sign the contract with K&F?

Task 5: Word power

1)	You don't seem to realise that ...	**d**	You seem to forget that ...
2)	As it stands, I would not be able to give the project my backing.	**c**	Without substantial changes, I cannot give the proposal my support.
3)	This proposal is completely unrealistic.	**b**	I'm afraid this all only half baked.
4)	Are you sure the proposal is feasible?	**a**	Are you really convinced that this proposal is going to work?

Task 6: Scrambled compromises repaired

Let's strike a compromise.
We are ready to meet you halfway.
That seems to be a reasonable compromise.
I think that would be perfectly acceptable.
We are prepared to make certain concessions.
I think it is still possible to strike a compromise.

Task 7: Guided translation

I'd like to begin by giving you an *overview of* the project.
I'll be developing the three *main parts* of our project.
If I might *suggest* something.
If we could *come back / return* to the point.
If I could *turn* to another subject.
I'm afraid all these projects are *half-baked.*

Chapter 14

Task 2: Brain test

1)	K&F have bought IMM.	/ F
2)	K&F are going to sell IMM to the Russians.	/ F
3)	K&F want to test IMM at this meeting.	T /
4)	Mr Zhukov knew why IMM is present at the meeting.	/ F
5)	The Russians want to buy 2,000 laptops for the collecting of information for Moscow.	/ F
6)	The Russians want to buy software for the transmission of data to Moscow.	T /

Task 3: Patch work

We seem to be talking at at *cross purposes*.
If I've *understood* you correctly, you're saying that ...
I'm afraid there seems to have been a *slight* misunderstanding.
I'm afraid I didn't quite *follow/catch* what you said about this robot.
If I might explain in more detail it would *clarify* the situation.
Would I be *right* in saying that this robot conducts meetings?
Perhaps I should make this *clearer* by saying ...
I'm afraid we weren't quite able to *catch/follow* what you were saying.
Am I right in *assuming* that IMM will control our discussion?
Now, what you said is that you need laptops. Is that *correct* so far?

Task 4: Word power

1) Are you saying that ...?	**c**	When you say ... do you mean ...?
2) If I've understood you correctly, you're saying that ...?	**d**	Would I be right in saying that ...?
3) I'm afraid we weren't quite able to catch what you were saying.	**a**	I'm afraid I didn't quite follow what you said about ...
4) With respect, that is not what I said.	**e**	We seem to be talking at cross purposes.

5)	Perhaps I should make this clearer by saying ...	**b**	Perhaps if I might explain in more detail it would clarify the situation.

Task 5: Guided translation

If I've understood you correctly, you're saying that ...
I'm afraid we weren't quite able *to catch* what you were saying.
Perhaps *I should* make *this clearer* by saying ...
I'm afraid I didn't *quite follow* what you said about ...
Perhaps if I *might explain* in more detail it would *clarify* the situation.
We seem *to be talking at cross purposes.*

Task 6: Scrambled clarifications

Am I right in assuming that this loud metal man will control our discussion?
I'm afraid there seems to have been a slight misunderstanding.
Allow me to rephrase that to make sure that I've understood you correctly.
Now, basically what you said is that you need two thousand pieces of software.
With respect, that is not what I said.
We seem to be talking at cross purposes.
I'm afraid I didn't quite follow what you said about your robot.
Perhaps if I might explain in more detail it would clarify the situation.

Glossary

Abkürzungen: n. = Substantiv, v. = Verb, AE = American English, BE = British English

A

abuse s.o.'s rights	jds. Rechte verletzen
acute	akut
add	hinzufügen
adequately effective	angemessen wirksam
adjust the distance	den Abstand regeln, anpassen
advertising agency	Werbeagentur
advertising sheets	Seiten, Bögen mit Anzeigen
air blast	Luftschwall
amplify	vergrößern, verstärken
anger	Ärger
announce	ankündigen
apologise	sich entschuldigen
apology	Entschuldigung
apply for a loan	einen Kredit beantragen
appointment	Termin, Verabredung
approach s.o.	an jdn. herantreten
argue	streiten; argumentieren
arise; questions arise	Fragen tauchen auf
arrow	Pfeil
assume	annehmen, vermuten
at this stage	zu diesem Zeitpunkt
attendee	Anwesende(r)
attitude	Einstellung, Haltung
aural stimulus	akustischer Stimulus
authoritarian	autoritär
available	vorhanden, verfügbar
avoid a pitfall	eine Falle umgehen
awake; be ~	wach sein
aware; be ~ of sth.	sich einer Sache bewußt sein

B

back s.o.	jdn. unterstützen
barrel	Faß
be too eager	zu eifrig sein
be into sth.	gerne haben, sehr mögen
beat, beat, beaten	schlagen, schlug, geschlagen

behaviour	Benehmen
below the belt	unter der Gürtellinie
bet	wetten
bite one's tongue	sich auf die Zunge beißen
bite, bit, bitten	beißen
black look; give s.o. a ~ ~	jdn. böse anblicken
blow one's own trumpet	sich selbst loben
boot	Kofferraum
bossy	herrisch, diktatorisch
break	Pause
brush up	aufpolieren
bumper	Stoßstange
burglar alarm	Alarmanlage
Burgundy	Burgunder (Rotwein)
by heart	auswendig

C

call a spade a spade	die Dinge beim Namen nennen
call it a day	Schluß machen
calm the situation down	die Wogen glätten
calm down	beruhige dich; sich beruhigen
cancel	streichen, absagen,
cash up	abkassieren
cash-cow	Melkkuh, Goldesel
catch a word	ein Wort verstehen
catch a pneumonia	sich Lungenentzündung holen
cease	enden; aufhören, einstellen
certain	sicher
check	prüfen
choice	(Aus-)Wahl
clank	klirren
clarification	Klarstellung
clarify	klarstellen, klären
come up with an idea	eine Idee haben
concerned, be ~ with	hier: interessiert an
confirmation	Bestätigung
connect the water	das Wasser anschließen
consider	betrachten, in Betracht ziehen

contribution	Beitrag
convince	überzeugen
couple (v.)	anschließen
court case	Gerichtsverhandlung
cover costs	Kosten abdecken
cross purposes; be at ~ ~	aneinander vorbeireden
curable	heilbar
cutting sense of humour	scharfer Sinn für Humor

D

deaf	taub
decision	Entscheidung
declare a meeting open/closed	eine Besprechung für eröffnet/für geschlossen erklären
depending on	abhängig von
depressed	deprimiert
desperate	verzweifelt
detect	entdecken
device	Gerät, Vorrichtung
disappointment	Enttäuschung
disciplinary action	disziplinarische Maßnahmen
disgusting	abscheulich
disposal; have sth. at one's ~	etwas zur Verfügung haben
distribute software	Software vertreiben
doctorate	Doktortitel
doom; voice of ~ has sounded	Schicksal; die Stimme des ~s hat gesprochen
double Dutch	Kauderwelsch
doubt	Zweifel
doze off	einnicken
draw attention to	die Aufmerksamkeit lenken auf
drawings	Zeichnungen
due to	wegen

E

efficiency	Effizienz, Leistungsfähigkeit
effort	Anstrengung, Mühe
eliminate	entfernen, ausschalten

elongated hose	verlängerter Schlauch
enemy	Feind
energised by	angetrieben durch
enterprise	Unternehmen
establish a company	eine Firma gründen
exaggerate	übertreiben
excessive amount of work	übermäßig viel Arbeit
expand	erweitern, verlängern
experience	Erfahrung

F

facilities	Möglichkeiten, Einrichtungen
Fancy!	Stell dir vor!
feasible	machbar
fidget	nervös herumfummeln
field; in this ~	auf diesem Gebiet
file a patent	ein Patent anmelden
file (n.)	Datei; Ordner
focus on	sich konzentrieren auf
foil	Folie
for my part	was mich angeht, meinerseits
foreign duty	Auslandsdienst
found a company	eine Firma gründen
frame	Rahmen
free of charge	umsonst
frighten the life out of s.o.	jdn. zu Tode erschrecken
from my point of view	aus meiner Sicht
funnel	Trichter

G

gadget	Apparat, Vorrichtung
gap	Lücke
gathering	Zusammenkunft
gear-wheel	Zahn-, Getrieberad
get s.o. to do sth.	jdn. dazu bringen, etw. zu tun
get side-tracked	hier: vom Thema abkommen
gift of speech	die Gabe der Sprache

give support	unterstützen
glad to have the chance	erfreut sein über die Gelegenheit
go along with s.o.	mit jemandem einverstanden sein
go for it	es anpacken
grant a patent	ein Patent erteilen
grant s.o. a loan	jdm. einen Kredit gewähren
grateful	dankbar
grunt	grunzen

H

hand-out	Tischvorlage
have complete confidence in s.o.	volles Vertrauen zu jdm. haben
have a lot of potential	hier: vielversprechend sein
have vision	Weitblick haben
have the honour of ...	die Ehre haben zu ...
he's in another league.	er ist in einer anderen Klasse.
head of investment	Leiter der Investitionsabteilung
hearing disabilities	Hörschäden
heavy; the ~ hand of the law	die schwere Hand des Gesetzes
heretofore	bis heute *(veraltet)*
hesitate	zögern
hidden flaw	der versteckte Fehler
hit (n.)	Treffer, Hit
hood (AE), bonnet (BE)	Motorhaube

I

implications	Folgen, Konsequenzen
impressive	eindrucksvoll
improvement	Verbesserung
in advance	im voraus
in addition to	zusätzlich zu
inability	Unfähigkeit
include	einschließen, umfassen
indigestion	Verdauungsstörung
indisposed	unpäßlich
insurance	Versicherung
interrupt	unterbrechen

intervene	eingreifen
introduce; ~ s.o.	jdn. vorstellen
introductory words	einführende Worte
invention	Erfindung
it went off very successfully	es war sehr erfolgreich
it was really a giggle	es war wirklich lächerlich
item one on the agenda	Punkt eins der Tagesordnung

J

join s.o.	sich jdm. anschließen

K

keen on	scharf auf
keep on track	bei der Sache bleiben, beim Thema bleiben
kinky	verrückt, pervers

L

laughing matter	etwas Lächerliches
law	Gesetz
lecture in linguistics	Vorlesung über Linguistik
legal aspects	juristische Aspekte
length	Länge
let me assure you	seien Sie versichert
light (n.)	Licht
look for	suchen nach
look forward to	sich freuen auf
lungs	Lungen

M

main parts	wichtige Teile
major functions	wichtige Funktionen
major	wichtig, bedeutend
mention	erwähnen
metal pipe	Metallrohr
minutes of the meetings	das Protokoll der Besprechung

mounted	montiert
movable parts	bewegliche Teile
my goodness!	du meine Güte!

N

namesake	Namensvetter
network link-up	Zugang/Verbindung zu einem Netzwerk
nine o'clock sharp	Punkt neun Uhr
noise	Geräusch, Lärm
non-starter	Versager, Niete

O

object to a plan	gegen einen Plan sein
occupant; the ~ of the bed	der im Bett Liegende
occur; it occurs to me	mir kommt der Gedanke; mir fällt auf/ein
on behalf of	im Namen von
on condition that	unter der Bedingung, daß
on approval	auf Probe
once upon a time	es war einmal
opinion	Meinung
opportunity	Gelegenheit
opportunity; take the ~ to	die Gelegenheit wahrnehmen zu
option	Wahl, Alternative
Order!	Ruhe!
over-authoritarian	zu autoritär
over-sensitive	überempfindlich
overview	Überblick
owner	Besitzer

P

pain	Schmerz
participant	Teilnehmer
pay off	sich lohnen
pay attention	aufpassen
peaceful	friedlich

performance	Leistung; Vorstellung
pillow	Kissen
pint; a couple of ~ s	ein paar Glas Bier
Pity about that idea!	Schade um die Idee!
placement	hier: Befestigung
please refer to the OHP sheet	betrachten Sie bitte die Folie
plod forward	sich durchkämpfen
pneumatic	pneumatisch, lufthydraulisch
pneumatics	Lufthydraulik
pneumonia	Lungenentzündung
pointer	Zeiger
polish sth. up	etw. aufpolieren
portable OHP	tragbarer Overheadprojektor
potential customer	möglicher Kunde
pour	gießen
practical matter	praktische Angelegenheit
practicalness	die praktische Seite
pre-conference handouts	Tischvorlagen, die vor der Besprechung verteilt werden
predetermined time	vorbestimmte Zeit
premises	Firmenräume, -gelände
prevent	verhindern
print	ausdrucken
process the text	den Text bearbeiten; hier: lesen
profit margin	Gewinnspanne
promote novels	für Romane werben
promotion	Werbung; Beförderung
pronounce	aussprechen
pronounciation	Aussprache
propose	vorschlagen
prosecute	gerichtlich belangen
protector	Beschützer
pull yourself together!	reiß' dich zusammen!
put s.o. out of work	jdn. arbeitslos machen
put s.o. right	jdn. korrigieren
put in an opposition	Widerspruch einlegen

R

raise one's glass to	sein Glas erheben auf
razor	Rasierer, Rasiermesser
reason (n.; v.)	Grund; argumentieren
receive	erhalten
reckon	annehmen, vermuten
rectangular outlet	rechteckige Öffnung
regarding that matter	was diese Sache anbelangt
regarding	betreffend
relative clause	Relativsatz
remind s.o. of sth.	erinnern; jdn. an etw. ~
report	hier: sich melden
represent	darstellen
rep (representative)	Vertreter
require	erfordern, verlangen, benötigen
research	Forschung
response	Reaktion
retract the bumper	die Stoßstange einziehen
revise	wiederholen
rotatable damper vane	drehbarer dämpfender Ventilator
rule	Regel, Vorschrift
run riot	Amok laufen

S

sacrifice (v.; n.)	opfern; Opfer
salary structure	Gehaltsstruktur
schedule; keep ~ s	Terminpläne einhalten
secret service	Geheimdienst
select	auswählen
self-confident	selbstbewußt
sensitivity	Empfindlichkeit
sheet	Bogen, Blatt
shift the chairs	die Stühle umstellen
sieve through	aussieben
sign	unterschreiben
simulated thunder	simulierter Donner
skills	Fähigkeiten

slam the door	die Tür zuschlagen
sophisticated	hochentwickelt
sort oneself out	sich Klarheit verschaffen
sort out the possibilities	die Möglichkeiten sichten
specifications	Spezifikationen
splendid	prächtig
squabble	Zank, Kabbelei
stage; at this ~	zu diesem Zeitpunkt
start-up loan	Anfangs-, Anschubkredit
statement	Aussage, Erklärung
step in	einspringen, aushelfen
step by step	Schritt für Schritt
stick to the subject	beim Thema bleiben
stomach-ache	Bauchweh
Stone me!	Ich werd' verrückt!
stress (v.; n.)	betonen; Betonung
stroke	Schlaganfall
subject	Thema, Gegenstand
subsidiary	Tochtergesellschaft
substantial changes	wesentliche Änderungen
succeed	erfolgreich sein, Erfolg haben
suck	saugen
suggest	vorschlagen, anregen
suggestion	Vorschlag
supplier	Lieferant
support (v.; n.)	unterstützen; Unterstützung
suppose	annehmen, vermuten
surface	Oberfläche
suspect	vermuten, argwöhnen
swallow	schlucken
switch	(um)schalten
swivel	sich drehen, schwenken

T

take the minutes	das Protokoll führen
talk over s.o.'s head	über jds. Kopf hinwegreden
tap	(Wasser-)Hahn
tap on the foil	auf die Folie klopfen

target/objective	Ziel
teething problems	Kinderkrankheiten
tentative	versuchsweise, vorsichtig
that's the pot calling the kettle black	ein Esel schilt den andern Langohr
The Wind in the Willows	Der Wind in den Weiden (Roman von T. Rattigan)
tooth rack	Zahnstange
touch; we'll be in ~	Sie hören von uns
tow away	abschleppen
town council	Stadt- / Gemeinderat
translate	übersetzen
transmit	übertragen, übermitteln
truth; the moment of ~	die Stunde der Wahrheit
turn to	sich zuwenden

U

UK (United Kingdom)	Vereinigtes Königreich von Großbritannien
unmentionables	die Unaussprechlichen (Unterhosen)
under lock and key	unter Dach und Fach
undertaking	Unternehmen, Vorhaben
unfounded	unbegründet
unleash s.o. on	jdn. loslassen auf
unsuspecting house-owners	nichtsahnende Hausbesitzer
upper right-hand corner	die obere rechte Ecke
upset	verwirrt, verstört, schockiert
upside down	verdreht, umgekehrt
usefulness	Nützlichkeit

V

vacuum cleaner	Staubsauger
value	Wert
valve	Ventil
various devices	verschiedene Geräte, Vorrichtungen
various	verschiedene
view	Ansicht

virgin	Jungfrau
voice	Stimme

W

wash-basin	Waschbecken
waste time	Zeit verschwenden
waterworks	hier: Wasserspiele
We've got the message.	Wir haben verstanden.
wet through	naß bis auf die Knochen
what's your feeling?	wie denkst du darüber?
windbag	Windbeutel, windiger Bursche
wonders never cease!	es gibt noch Zeichen und Wunder
worthless suggestion	wertloser Vorschlag

3667/5